Arsen Rubenovich Arakelyan
Tamara Akopyan

Television and documentary filmmaking

Arsen Rubenovich Arakelyan
Tamara Akopyan

Television and documentary filmmaking

The Journalist's Role in Making a Documentary

ScienciaScripts

Imprint

Any brand names and product names mentioned in this book are subject to trademark, brand or patent protection and are trademarks or registered trademarks of their respective holders. The use of brand names, product names, common names, trade names, product descriptions etc. even without a particular marking in this work is in no way to be construed to mean that such names may be regarded as unrestricted in respect of trademark and brand protection legislation and could thus be used by anyone.

Cover image: www.ingimage.com

This book is a translation from the original published under ISBN 978-620-2-09556-3.

Publisher:
Sciencia Scripts
is a trademark of
Dodo Books Indian Ocean Ltd. and OmniScriptum S.R.L Publishing group
Str. Armeneasca 28/1, office 1, Chisinau-2012, Republic of Moldova, Europe
Printed at: see last page
ISBN: 978-620-5-32564-3

CONTENTS

INTRODUCTION

Film, television, journalism. What is the connection between them? Cinema was born to perpetuate reality. Throughout the history of cinema, it has not only captured reality, but also offered its own interpretation of reality. It was the first films that we can call documentaries. As strange as it may seem now, they were of a television nature even before the advent of television itself. The films of the pioneers of cinema, the Lumière brothers, were in a "no comment" format: when the camera in the film showed a still frame with no movement, no editing and no off-screen text. This was pure documentary filmmaking. The documentary film genre shows life as it is. Documentary is not only a kind of cinematography, but also a link between cinema, television and journalism. One of the key features of documentary filmmaking is its unpredictability. Documentary filmmaker captures reality without fiction, but at the same time using the artistic means of cinematography. Television, in turn, has enormous possibilities of documenting reality. It is a synthesis of various types of art, but it is film that is closest to it. It is impossible to unequivocally answer the question of whether television is art or whether it is more like a large factory where various genre specific products are produced. The main mission of journalistic work is to show real events, phenomena, and to inform objectively. Thus, the journalist plays an essential role in the creation of a documentary on television, acting in the role of the author.

In the thesis we investigated the stages of formation and development of cinematography, focusing on documentary films.

As the famous screenwriter and film theorist Bela Balasz states in his work, there are three phenomena that are necessary to create a film: a frame (close-up), a foreshortening and editing. It is through close-ups, foreshortening and montage that cinema acquires its own special language. The close-up shows us phenomena in such close proximity that we would never see them in reality with the naked eye. It is only in the frame that the director's subjective field of vision is revealed. Because of this, the dramatic content of the scene acquires a special composition in the frame, and we can only see this through the camera. And finally, it is only through editing that the composition of the entire work is built.

These three basic elements are what a journalist uses in his or her work and produce what is called a documentary. We are really interested in documentary filmmaking, because it is the documentary film that can be a powerful weapon in the hands of a journalist to reveal various phenomena of reality.

The focus of our research work is on the specifics of journalistic work in the process of creating a documentary film. We have also studied several television journalistic genres that most incorporate elements of documentary filmmaking and have put the focus on the specifics of the modern television film. We also paid attention to the ethical and moral principles of a journalist acting in the role of a documentary filmmaker.

Along with the theoretical part of the study in the practical part through our own film we show not only the practical work done in recent months, but also the work for 3 years. Consequently, our own documentary film shows how a future journalist can learn from his mistakes year after year and, starting from simple reports, reach the creation of an author's program, which contains many elements of documentary.

Relevance of the topic:

Today, almost all the best television reports include elements of film. Journalists try to make their video sequences as expressive and entertaining as possible. A good reporter, like a film director, is distinguished by his unconventional view of what is happening and by his ability to discern all the most interesting details in it. In this way, contemporary television production can have a strong impact on a wide audience. We hear various human stories today that, thanks to journalistic work, are turned into documents of eternity.
It is the documentation of these many stories that brings to light many universal problems of humanity.

Novelty of the study:

Due to increasing technological progress and the formation of a digital society, television is also developing at a rapid pace. To date, compared to television, the Internet is not yet sufficiently mass-marketed. Television has always had a regular audience and has every possible way of influencing society. In the vast number of documentaries on television, you have to choose the quality ones and lead the journalists in the right direction, because the present and future of documentary films is television.

Subject of the study:

"Television and Documentary. The Journalist's Role in Making a Documentary".
The object of the study:

The relationship of the documentary to television and the activities of the journalist, features of documentaries and television films.

Purpose and objectives of the work:

To show the inseparable connection between documentary filmmaking and television and journalism. To create one's own documentary on the basis of theoretical and methodological research, existing examples of films and one's own journalistic practice. In order to achieve this goal, it is necessary to:

1. Find the distinctive features of a television documentary
2. To study the specifics of non-fiction films on the example of classic and contemporary documentaries
3. Find out what role a journalist plays in the making of a documentary
4. To study the history of Armenian documentary cinema
5. Predict trends in the further development of documentary film on television
6. Make the result of the research work the creation of their own documentary film.

Structure of the work:

Our thesis consists of an introduction, three chapters, and a conclusion. The first chapter tells about the emergence and the way of formation of cinematography. In it we also consider the varieties and genre features of cinema. In Chapter II, we study the special features and types of documentaries and television, the characteristics of journalists' work in creating documentaries, and we devote a separate section to Armenian documentary filmmaking. In Chapter III we examine current trends in television and the specific journalistic genres that most often contain elements of documentaries.

In the conclusion we give the conclusions of our research work, as well as telling about the scenario of our own reporting documentary.

CHAPTER 1. THE ORIGINS OF CINEMATOGRAPHY

1.1. History of the emergence of cinematography

Cinema is designed to perpetuate reality. It has tremendous power to influence human perception. Before the birth of cinema there was no art that could show reality so comprehensively and be as close to human life as it was. And although the art of theater played a huge role in the first films, actors played the same way as on stage, strongly gesturing and giving the face more expression so as not to feel the lack of speech, cinema is still different in its technique. If initially it seemed to most people only technical means of fixing reality and a way of reproducing a work of art (we mean theater, painting, literature), then over time the cinema created a new way of depicting reality: its language, editing system, camera thinking, new expressive art actor. It is not without reason that cinema is called the offspring of technological progress. It has play, light and color, word, music, noise, sounds, composition, different plans and the three most important things, which are unique to it - the frame, the perspective and montage. The same thing happened in TV. Initially it emerged as a mass medium, combining all the possibilities of newspapers, radio, newsreels and even the direct speech of the propagandist. But here, too, the phenomenon of television art developed over time on the basis of technology. TV not only transmits through its channels a play or a film, but also creates what is called a television play and a telefilm[2] . Cinema came into existence at the end of the 19th century. Although before its birth, in the first half of the 19th century, there was already a medium for capturing reality, or more specifically, still images. We are talking about photography. Many of today's photographers also believe that photography plays a huge role in capturing reality. For example, Georgie Gerzina Powells. The photographer believes that photography (especially non-commercial photography) is, indeed, a way of showing the world. But there is a subtlety here. She doesn't just show the world, she shows it exactly through the eyes of the author:

"Every photograph is a part of the author, something he loves or hates."[3]

It is not without reason that the photographer prefers street photography most of all, as

---

[2] Freilich S. I. Film Theory: from Eisenstein to Tarkovsky, 2005.
[3] Georgie Gerzina Pauels: Life itself makes street photography fascinating//Jao8Ryo1o.com, 08.12.2015//http://www.rosphoto.com/interview/dzhordzhi dzherzina pauels-4221

the most natural, unpredictable and unexpected photos are taken outdoors. She is attracted by the authenticity of photography. This is what life and reality are like when they are captured through film, through the eyes of a director. This is the main similarity between photography and cinema. Of course, it took a huge effort to create cinema: the pioneers of cinema were not able to invent technology right away. Today, modern technology is already available and, with a simple camera, it's easy to shoot the shots you want. It often seems to us that everything is easy and simple, there is nothing unusual about it. But there was a time when scientists and professors spent many years of their lives and sacrificed themselves to understand the circuitry of the smallest details of the equipment that serves us today. One such example in the history of cinema is the Plato Victim phenomenon.

Belgian professor Joseph Plato, who in the summer of 1829 in Liège made a risky experiment and for 25 seconds, without taking his eyes off the red-hot disk of the midday sun, in order to find out the limit of resistance of the human retina, as a result of which he goes blind. Plato spends the following days in a dark room, after which he gradually regains his sight. The professor did not stop there and continued his experiments in optics, and in 1842 he became permanently blind. In 1832 he finally succeeds in creating a small device that contained all the basic principles of cinema. This device was called a fenakistiscope.[4]

An interesting fact is that almost simultaneously with Plato's invention, Simon von Stampfer, a professor at the Vienna Polytechnic, invented a device called the "stroboscope", which was very similar to Plato's phenakistiscope. The funny thing is that both professors did not know about each other's experiments and simultaneously got the same result each in their own way.

Many attempts have been made to create a system for recording and reproducing moving images. American inventor and entrepreneur Thomas Edison and his engineer William Dixon invented two devices, the "kinetograph" and the "kinetoscope," one of which recorded motion and the other showed it[5] . Their first session took place on April 14, 1894. Still, the device they invented remained only a commonplace attraction and was designed for individual viewing only. Edison's attempts to take his place among the masters of the world and become an industrialist led him to exploit his inventions and after that he did not invent

---

[4] Sadoul J. General History of Cinema. Volume 1. Chapter 1. Joseph Plato lays the foundations of cinema. Moscow: Art, 1958.

[5]   Sadoul J. General History of Cinema. Volume 1. Chapter VIII. Edison - the inventor of film// http://coollib.eom/b/260867/read#t13

anything serious.

A first important and significant step in the history of cinema was taken by the French-born brothers Louis and Auguste Lumière. As a result, they were recognized as the inventors of the cinematograph. The Lumières' device was called the "Cinematograph" or "Cinematograph." With the Lumière apparatus, it was easy to shoot and show motion pictures on the big screen. In March 1895 the first public screening took place in Paris, but the birthday of cinema is considered December 28th, 1895. On that day the first commercial screening took place in the basement of the Grand Café on the Boulevard des Capucines.[6]

The most famous of the short Lumière commercials they showed to the public was called "Arrival of a Train. Probably the strongest impression of the reel had to do with the sensation of the moving train coming toward the audience, which is why the reel looked very realistic to the audience. The Lumière sessions consisted of short clips that lasted 50 seconds. They showed different kinds of movements. For example, they showed waves of the sea, blacksmiths working, different street scenes, and the destruction of a wall which was rebuilt at the end of the reel. One of these early clips showed Auguste Lumiere and his wife spoon-feeding an infant who was sitting at a table between them. The first film they made, titled "Workers Walking Out of the Factory," usually began the film session. First the women in hats and workers' dresses would come out of the factory, and then the men, an officer with a dog, a man on a bicycle. All this together in the frame looks very realistic, like all the other films - domestic scenes, which in those days even intimidated the viewer with their realism. One of Lumiere's most popular features, along with "Arrival of the Train," is considered to be "The Watering Man." It was the first film that was staged and had the completeness of a narrative structure. A man is watering a garden with a hose, a boy sneaks up to him and steps on the hose behind him, the waterman stands and wants to understand what happened, he looks at the tip of the hose, the boy takes his foot away and the jet of water hits him in the face. He hits the boy, and the latter runs away. It turns out that the movie, which lasts 37 seconds, has an exposition, a plot, a climax, and a denouement. A film where there is a simple story. It was this picture that set the beginning of feature films in cinematic history. Frames of Lumière films are considered masterpieces in the history of cinema because of their simplicity and naturalness.

An interesting fact is that we see the same footage these days on various TV channels

---

[6]   Ibid. Chapter XIII. Lumière Brothers Cinematography// http://eoollib.eom/b/260867/read#t18

when, for example, we watch the news in the evening. The same fire that firefighters are trying to put out, the work of some factory employees and many other everyday situations and incidents. On the one hand, the same report is as close to reality as possible and reflects life itself, but on the other hand, the report has the subjective perception of the journalist, he becomes a participant and witness of the event.[7]

It turns out that the director here is a journalist who himself often appears in the frame with a stand-up to make everything look even more natural.

1.2. The initial period of film development

After the Lumières, cinema was given a new expression thanks to a 35-year-old young man, Georges Méliès, who transformed it from an amusing scientific novelty into a new genre of spectacle. He himself was the director of the Théâtre Robert-Oudin in the heart of Paris, was an excellent magician, drew caricatures, created sets and costumes for the theater, often played leading roles in plays himself, combined theatrical mise-en-scène and techniques and created an entirely new genre in cinema. However, his first films were imitations of Lumière's paintings. Even the titles of these films said so, such as Arrival of a Train in Vincennes, The Waterman, Children and Young Girls, Sea Scenes, and War Scenes. But then, after one unexpected but simple incident that occurred while shooting a street scene in Paris, everything changed.

He himself tells how, while filming Opera Square, there was a delay in the machine, and while he freed up space on the film and started the machine up again, passersby, crews and everyone else changed their places. As he projected the tape at the spot where the breakup occurred, Méliès saw that suddenly men turned into women and other characters into many other interesting things. After this happy accident, he began filming his first tricks: the transformation of men into women and disappearances. At first he used the presence of a magician in the frame. Soon he realized that he could already film one of his theater numbers, "The Abduction of the Lady." In the picture, Méliès is in a magician's costume with a lady sitting on a chair. He covers the lady with cloth, does his magic manipulation, and the woman disappears, and then she reappears. In fact, the shooting would stop, Méliès would freeze in place, and the lady would quickly run away. Then the shooting continued again. But when

---

[7] Kuznetsov G.V., Tsvik V.L., Yurovsky A.Y. Television journalism. Chapter VIII. Genres of television journalism, 2002. //http://evartist.narod.ru/text6/32.htm

viewing the picture, the stop is not noticeable at all. He was able to make it so that the viewer had a complete illusion. He also used the trick of speed shooting in his experiments.[8]

The interest in Méliès' films was enormous, and he enjoyed great success with the public. He introduced many new genres - comedies, skits with stunts, extravaganzas, reconstructions of events ("The Taking of Tournavos," "The Execution of the Spy," "Battles in the Streets of India"). He made 60 films of 20 meters each. Also 16 comic scenes, "The American Surgeon," "The Imaginary Sick Man," and "The Drunkard's Dream." These short jokes are notable for their sets, costumes, and actors. He uses his tricks of transformation in the fairies "The Hypnotist," "The Devil's House," and "The Alchemist's Hallucinations." The most famous among them is "The Cabinet of Mephistopheles," where he himself appears in the costume of Mephistopheles, and his image perfectly suits the role. Méliès is also known for his narrative films. Among his most recent is The Dreyfus Affair, which lasted more than a quarter of an hour. He made entire operas, such as Faust, filmed in 1904, in which he made nothing up as he liked to capture theatrical reality. And so the "Méliès era" continues until 1902. He leaves a tremendous influence on his followers and is truly considered the father of modern film.

In 1902 he released his masterpiece, A Trip to the Moon. Méliès combined the works of Jules Verne and Herbert Wells, From the Earth to the Moon and The First Men on the Moon. The giant cannon, the madmen's club, and all the lunar episodes: the blizzard, the battle with the Selenites, the descent into the lunar crater, the arrival at the bottom of the ocean are taken from the first.[9]

The director's imagination is striking in this film, and the various costumes and sets in the first place made it a success and a masterpiece. And speaking of how the news of the film's success spread throughout France and Europe, the day after its success Méliès received orders from all over France. The production of the film cost him 10 thousand francs, and his next famous film "The Coronation of King Edward VII of England" - 80 thousand francs, which was given to him by the "Warwick Film" company Urbana. After this film, the king said that the funniest thing about the story was that he recognized himself and the queen, and if he didn't know beforehand that they weren't, he would have thought they were the ones

---

[8]   Sadoul J. General History of Cinema. Volume 1. Chapter XIV. Georges Méliès - creator of the cinematic spectacle// http://coollib.com/b/260867/read#t33

[9]   Sadoul J. General History of Cinema. Volume 1. Chapter XIII. Journey to the moon// http://eoollib.eom/b/260867/read#t50

being filmed.

From 1903-1909, cinema transformed from a craft into a major industry. During this period the world cinema is no longer led by the artist, but by the industrialist Charles Pathet[10] . He was not only a manufacturer, but also the head of an enterprise. He made apparatuses, films, and later he began to build studios, mechanical workshops, copy factories, and opened branches abroad. But he is not satisfied with all this and wants to monopolize the distribution and screening of all films. But France, an economically less developed country than the United States, would not be able to hold a monopoly in its hands in the world film industry. From 1908 - 1909 years in the U.S. there are already thousands of movies, while in France there were only a few hundred. In Italy, on the other hand, societies were founded that would sooner or later compete with Pate, despite the fact that here cinema had partly emerged from Pate's own enterprises. In England during the same period there are also changes in the film industry. While the English were formerly famous for their comedies and dramas, now they are already making a great contribution to the development of documentaries and scientific films. The director of Warwick Film, Charles Urban, leaves the firm and opens his own company, Urban Trading Company. The firm begins distributing films by the Lumières, Méliès, Smith, and Mottershaw, and produces only documentaries and science films itself. It also produced films about travel. Of this series were "Alps in Winter," "Picturesque Switzerland," and "Climbing the Serven." The latter was one of the first mountaineering films. And of the famous documentaries were "Business Bees," "Etudes from Natural History," "The Invisible World," and "Sea Fauna." These films were made by Professor Martin Duncan. When the films were shown at the 1903 Alhambra, Urban's slogan was "Nature on Stage!" The films included such pictures as a battle between a fly and a spider, red blood globules in a frog's leg, various freshwater hydras, and infusoria. To make "From Cape of Good Hope to Cairo," the cameraman paddled over rapids on a 100-meter-long rope to film the Victoria Falls on the Zambezi River. Also a great success was the film A Celebration in Delhi, which showed the coronation of Edward VII as Emperor of India. "Social" realism was also common in English cinema. One such striking example is Jams Williamson's Wait Until Jack Comes Home.

Thus, gradually with economic development, technology is also developing. Film factories and cinemas appear everywhere. The company "Gomon" builds a cinematographic

---

[10] Ibid. Chapter 2. Pate creates a film industry trust// http://coollib.eom/b/260867/read#t52

theater in 1905. The existence of such a theater (studio), makes it possible to shoot genre and comic scenes, staged movies, thanks to the huge size of the studio and the availability of the latest mechanical devices. The Edison and Pate studios were also famous. When it was necessary to shoot at night, the studios made it possible to use artificial light instead of sunlight. And so, instead of manual labor, sophisticated mechanical devices are used. Sales of filming and projection equipment are growing tremendously. The demand for new equipment is growing.

We can not talk about the pioneers of cinema and not mention the journey of David W. Griffith. His life was not easy, even from a young age he had to make a living: he worked as a newspaperman, laborer, metal worker, elevator operator, librarian and even a fireman. And then he specialized in character roles, playing Abraham Lincoln and many other characters.

The 32-year-old Griffith finally applied to various studios and began working at the Bayograph. He did not consider himself a good actor, he most of all loved the business of writing. Lee Daugherty of "Byograf" accepted his script "Old Loaner Isaac." After that, he stayed at Bayograph and played various roles with his wife. He soon found he looked ridiculous in front of the machine and decided never to act again. He continued to write movie scripts. He made his first film, The Adventures of Dolly, in 1908. The film's script was written by Stanner Tayler and was not that important. The story is about a little girl, Dolly, who is kidnapped by gypsies and hidden in a barrel. The barrel falls and rolls right into the river. But Dolly is rescued by a fisherman and gets her out of there. One of the features of the film was that it first starred a young actor, whom Griffith meets on the street and, struck by his appearance, learning that he is an actor, invites him to star in his film. The film was a success, which was followed by other films of the author. He soon became the main director of Bayograph.[11]

He made a lot of American minute comedies, but then other directors started doing it. His second film was Redskin and Child, which was shot at Little Falls, New Jersey. His next studio film was "Out of Love for Gold," based on short stories by writer Jack London. The film is about two bandits who try to steal from one another and put poison in each other's coffee. At the end, they die at the table, sitting against each other. Griffith didn't use a lot of

---

[11]   Sadoul J. General History of Cinema. Volume 1. Chapter XIX. Griffith's beginnings at the Bayograph // http://coollib.eom/b/260867/read#t70

scenery, with a table and two cups of coffee in the frame. Thus, he wanted all the viewer's interest to be directed to the expressions of the two actors' faces, so Griffith systematically introduced close-ups of the actors' faces. Soon he reached a point where he could already invite actors and recruit the cast of "Byograf. The heroine of his everyday comedies was actress Florence Lawrence ("The Girl and the Villain," "Love the Jewess," "Treacherous Fingerprints," "The Taming of the Shrew," "Backstage," "The Way of the Woman"), which, together with his special technique of installation was the reason for the success of Griffith films. He used montage contrasting short scenes that took place simultaneously in different places. But it was not the movement of the characters in space that bound these scenes together, but the commonality of thought of the dramatic action. If Méliès used montage, close-ups, movement of the apparatus, the swoop, but considered it all a theatrical trick and a magical device of directing, Griffith turned it all into a means of dramatic expression. Méliès likened the screen to a stage where the actors' faces are seen from a distance and poorly concealed by makeup. Griffith allowed the viewer to be face to face with the actor. He brought continuity of action to film, his device was able to penetrate everywhere. Griffith brings movie stars to the movies, the viewer begins to already remember the faces of the actors. In the cinema, as in the theater, can not be already made up faces of actors, it does not have to play in masks.

And so it was said above that the three most important phenomena in cinema are the frame (close-up), the foreshortening, and the editing.

In his book "The ABCs of Directing" the famous Soviet film director Lev Kuleshov defines the frame in great detail. A frame is every cell of the film on which an image is shot. But sometimes it's hard to distinguish when the old frame ends and the new one begins. It happens that a cell changes, there are frames that can completely change the composition of the frame.[12]

For example, in Federico Fellini's Amarcord, a single frame can last five minutes or even longer. Within the frame there are modifications, it is equipped with sounds, music, noises, conversations of the crowd, in which there are people from all different walks of life, but during this time the frame does not change.

This is the main feature of the frame. And the foreshortening is, first of all, the director's point of view. For example, if he wants to show the poor woman in the frame more

---

[12]   Kuleshov L. The ABCs of Film Direction. Moscow: Art, 1969. C. 8-9

depressed, so that it would be pity to look at her, he takes the upper foreshortening and shows her from above.[13]

Whereas in painting or photography the author takes one point and it remains unchanged, in cinema the perspective can change all the time. Montage, in turn, is a very important creative and technical element in the creation of a picture. Not only does montage glue together different shots, plans, and logical, sequential actions, but it also shows the director's attitude to what was shot.

Since we are talking about editing, it is essential to mention the Soviet director Sergei Eisenstein. There is hardly a contemporary who does not know Eisenstein's name. He was an artist who united and portrayed the masses at the most pivotal and decisive moments in history (from "The Stachka" to "Ivan the Terrible").[14]

For him, reality itself is nothing. In his films he does not just show the events of reality, but his main goal is to influence the viewer through the form in which this reality is presented. What matters is how the film is perceived by the audience. Based on this principle, Eisenstein creates the theory of "attraction montage. An attraction is understood as a demonstrated fact, object, or phenomenon that acts on the attention and psyche of the viewer. How the director presents these phenomena to achieve the desired result is another matter. He must juxtapose the images, create associations which together would cause a certain effect in people. This is actually Eisenstein's main method. He obtained the desired result through montage. And it is no coincidence that in his article entitled "Bela Forgetting Scissors" he writes about the position of film theorist Bela Balash and accuses him of not paying enough attention in his theory to such an important phenomenon as montage[15].

Eisenstein could have been anything - an engineer, an artist, a writer, an art historian, a teacher, but he became a filmmaker because this profession expresses the unifying ability of the creator. Cinema is a kind of polyphony in creativity. Perhaps if the technological progress of the Renaissance had been at the level at which it was in the late 19th century, such famous sculptors and artists of the time, as were Michelangelo, Leonardo da Vinci, along with their creations necessarily would have created "motion pictures" and "film sculptures". A

---

[13]   Ibid. C. 15-18

[14]   Freilich S. I. Film Theory: from Eisenstein to Tarkovsky. Moscow: Academic Project: Alma Mater. 2005. C. 250-251

[15]   Eisenstein S. M. Bela forgets the scissors//1ea1t-11b.gi// http://teatr-lib.ru/Library/Eisenstein/Select 2/# Toc319420505

striking example of this is Salvador Dali, who in addition to his surrealist paintings and sculptures, also created a kind of motion pictures.

From the birth of cinema until the advent of sound, the era of silent cinema continued. Each director brought new expressive means into the world of cinema, and this contributed enormously to the further development of cinema, but there were no words in the films. The actors' performance was accompanied by music, performed by pipers or guest orchestras. In order to supplement the lack of speech, there is a more expressive game of actors: mimics, gestures, movements, all together becoming close to the genre of comedy. American cinema 1920's has huge achievements in the genre of comedy. The pioneer of the American comedy is Mack Sennett. Although elements of comedy are still considered in Lumiere's films. A prime example is the film The Watered Man. But back to Sennet and his "slapstick" - farcical films that largely privileged the tradition of circus stunts. Here everything was built on the conflict of the man with the surrounding object environment. But the man himself had no special significance. Gradually, with the development of American film comedy, the comic character acquires its own character, which contributes to the film also had a philosophical sound. Famous representatives of the genre - Charles Chaplin and Buster Keaton, who does not fit in with human civilization and tries in every way to turn the circumstances in their favor. Keaton's character always knows in advance that all his attempts are doomed, but still considers it his duty to take risks ("Three eras", "Sherlock Jr.", "The General", "Cameraman"). The phenomenon of Chaplin is worth talking about separately ("Kid", "Gold Rush", "Circus"). As Kukarkin says in the preface to his book "Charlie Chaplin," his name has long been a household name. Chaplin and his character Charlie have merged for all into a single image that expresses specific ideas, concepts and notions[16] . Like Cervantes in literature, Chaplin in cinema created a tragicomic hero who is close to every heart and mind. They became, so to speak, people-masks, whom the viewer would never call just one-type actors (such actors were also Frunzik Mkrtchyan and Leonid Yengibarov). Film director and People's Artist of the USSR V. Pudovkin wrote that Chaplin belongs to the number of artists who become "masters of hearts". Chaplin lived for forty years in the United States and from the very beginning he found himself in conflict with Hollywood and all that he represented. And after years of political accusations, slander, film bans, scandalous lawsuits, and provocations, Chaplin was banished from the states after all. Probably only a great deal of

---

[16]   Kukarkin A. V. Charlie Chaplin. Moscow: Art, 1960. C. 4

popular love saved him from prison bars. He was indeed a genius. Chaplin's example is unparalleled in the history of world cinema. He is the principal actor, screenwriter, director of photography, director of editing and, with the advent of sound, also the composer of his films. Soon his imitation became a real profession. His first imitator was Billy Ricci. And then there were other fake Charlie Chaplins who filled circuses, musicals, and screens. He is still being imitated to this day. All of this speaks to the historical significance of his work. Charles Spencer Chaplin is a classic of world cinema.

No matter how long the era of silent cinema lasted, the fateful moment in the history of cinema came when sound was to appear. Although many famous directors and actors were against sound cinema, arguing that the presence of sound would interfere with their visual experiments, the advent of sound in cinema was inevitable. Chaplin, for his part, spoke humorously about it:

"It's a pity about silent movies after all. What a pleasure it was to see a woman open her mouth and not hear her voice!"[17]

What he really meant by these words was his deep regret. He didn't want the expressive performance of actors to suffer because of the advent of sound. But sound quickly earned its place in cinema, and during the 1930s almost all films became sound. Of course, the advent of sound reinforces the role of dialogue, which is the main content and expression of films. The first sound film in the history of cinema appears in 1927. Warner Bros. Company decides to take a risk and releases the first film in which the character speaks on the screen. The film was called The Jazz Singer. Admittedly, the film is more like a musical, as only the song is played, with which the actors convey their thought, while maintaining expressive acting and facial expressions. And in other parts of the film, the dialogues between the characters are again presented to the viewer in subtitles.

Unlike sound, color came more slowly to cinema. The first simple color film came out as early as 1922, but did not leave much of an impression on the viewer. The first full color short film appeared in 1934 by Technicolor under the title "La Cucaracha". Well, in 1935 the first full-length color film "Becky Sharp" was made by Ruben Mamulan, an American director of Armenian origin. Subsequently, this year is considered the year of the appearance of color cinema. Ruben Mamoulian was a real phenomenon in Hollywood. He began shooting "Cleopatra" starring Elizabeth Taylor, he directed the film "Queen

---

[17]   Kukarkin A. V. Charlie Chaplin. Moscow: Art, 1960. C. 5

Christina"[18] . He was the first in the history of cinema to use voice-over as the main character's inner monologue in a film, he also moved filming from the pavilion to the streets, he even wrote a book for children. In the 1980s, Ruben Mamoulian's name was inducted into the Broadway Hall of Fame. One of the stories of this genius' life so appealed to Sergei Dovlatov that he used it in one of his short stories.

The first Soviet color film called Grunya Kornakova appeared in 1936. Of the first color films, Gone with the Wind, shot in the United States in 1939, won great popularity with the public. Later technological advances have gone even further. Since the 1950s, the quality of film has gradually improved: its light sensitivity has risen. Magnetic recording is developed, new kinds of cinematography appear (panoramic, multiscreen, stereoscopic). All this leads to an improvement in the quality of film presentation. Gradually they began to talk about the effect of the viewer's presence.

1.3. Varieties and Genre Features of Cinema

It is interesting that the problem of genres has never been at the center of attention of film scholars, no matter how much interest in it is periodically exacerbated. After all, they emerged almost from the birth of cinema. Since cinema began as a chronicle, the problem of its natura and documentality absorbed the researchers.

However, the documentary nature of the film did not preclude its genre focus, but, on the contrary, suggested it. A striking example of this is Eisenstein's The Stachka, in which the action develops in the style of a chronicle, but, at the same time, there are also episodes that reach the point of eccentricity.[19]

In this regard, the documentary filmmaker Dziga Vertov argued with Eisenstein, believing that he was mixing feature film with documentary style. Eisenstein criticized Vertov for mixing newsreel with acting and editing episodes according to the laws of art. In fact, they both sought the same result - to overcome the old melodramatic art and come into direct contact with reality. It turns out that the genre and the documentary nature of the film are not mutually exclusive. On the contrary, they are deeply connected to the problem of method and

---

[18]   Hollywood pioneer Ruben Mamulyan from Tbilisi/NovostiNK//19.03.2016,11:40// http://novostink.ru/diaspora/148830-gollivudskiy-pioner-ruben-mamulyan-iz-tbilisi.html//

[19]   Freilich S. I. Film Theory: From Eisenstein to Tarkovsky. Moscow: Academic Project: Alma Mater. 2005. C. 40-45

the individual style of the director. The choice of film genre itself is already dependent on the director's style. Here he already shows his attitude to the event taking place and his view of life. In essence, genre is the director's individual style. Belinsky, in his article "On the Russian Novel and on Gogol's Stories" published in 1988 in Sovremennik, wrote about the author's individuality, comparing it to the color of the glasses through which he looks at the world:

"But there is also another originality arising from the author's individuality, a consequence of the color of the glasses through which he looks at the world. This originality in Mr. Gogol consists in comic animation, always overcome by a sense of deep sadness.[20]

Chaplin's genius was apparent in this. He himself cited an example from his own film "The Adventurer," where he is sitting on a balcony with a young girl and eating ice cream, while downstairs at the table is a venerable and very well dressed woman

woman. Eating ice cream, he drops a piece, which, having melted, flows down his pantaloons and falls on the lady's neck. The first burst of laughter is caused by the actor's awkwardness in this situation, and the second burst of laughter is the ice cream falling on the neck of the lady, who begins to yell and jump up and down. Chaplin was above all a good student of the thinking of the people for whom the film is intended. He considered two properties of human nature: first, the pleasure the audience feels when it sees the richness and brilliance of humiliation; second, the audience itself tends to experience the same feelings the actor feels. If he were to, say, drop an ice cream on the neck of a poor woman, a humble housewife, it would arouse not laughter but sympathy for her. Besides, the housewife has nothing to lose in terms of her dignity, and consequently nothing funny would result. And when the ice cream falls on the neck of a rich woman, the audience thinks that's the way to go. That's how Charles explains the specificity of his comedy. Eisenstein liked to experiment with genres. When he taught his students the techniques of directing, he repeated the same situation in a comedy, then in a drama. It can become both comedic and dramatic, but it depends on the content of the work and its idea.

There are not only purely cinematic genres, like the Western or comedy, but also those genres that cinema has adopted from other arts. These genres have not acquired other names, but certainly differ in their cinematic specificity. The novel becomes a cinematic novel, the novella becomes a cinematic sermon, the drama becomes a cinematic drama, the

---

[20]   Belinsky V.G. Vzglyad na russkoy literatury. On the Russian novel and on Gogol's novels, Sovremennik, 1988. //http://az.lib.ru/b/belinskij w g/text 0320.shtml

comedy becomes a cinematic comedy, etc. The younger and more contemporary art of cinema immediately began to form genres. Whereas in literature they emerged only as a result of long development. It was as if cinema combined the plastic spatiality of painting and the development of action over time that is characteristic of literature. Indeed, genres in cinema emerged almost with the birth of cinema. And no matter how they change, no matter how casually they collide with one another, they still retain their generic significance. M. Bakhtin writes that the genre always retains undying elements of archaicism. But this archaicism is preserved thanks to its constant renewal and, so to speak, updating:

"Genre is always this and that, old and new at the same time. Genre lives in the present, but always remembers its past, its beginning.[21]

It is also worth talking about purely cinematic genres. First of all, we need to be clear about what genre is. We can assume that genre is a definition applicable to any kind of art. Genre defines the characteristic features and differences in the structure of one work from another.

To the same genre can be attributed a lot of films that have similar features.

M. M. Bakhtin made an enormous contribution to the development of the theory of genres. He understands genre as a "typical form of the whole work" and speaks of the internal dialogicality of genres. By this he means that a work of art (namely a literary work) is also a form of "social communication. The living forces in the work are the author-creator, the hero created by the author, and the audience (reader, listener). According to the author, a work is always a "living statement. It is an active participant in the social dialogue. Genre is a kind of intermediary between the author and the audience (writer and reader).[22]

In each era, works are aimed at different types of readers, listeners, and audiences. All of this is also considered in the art of cinema. The director, when choosing a genre, first has to take into account the preferences and interests of the audience. In early Hollywood, an entire studio could specialize in one particular genre of film. For example, Paramount Pictures specialized in comedies, Universal Studios specialized in horror films, and Metro- Goldwyn-Mayer produced musicals. Today no film studio or director specializes in a particular genre. But because film ideas are often not clear and unambiguous and focused, film genres simply merge. This also happens from the diversity of genres. The filmmaker must be clear about what the purpose of the film is

---

[21]   Bakhtin. M. Problems of Dostoevsky's Poetics, Moscow: Khudozhestvennaya literatury, 1963. C. 141-142
[22]   Ibid.

and what audience it is aimed at. The viewer can better understand the division of feature films according to the subject matter of reflection. If we consider film comedies, the first films in the history of cinema were comic. This was probably due to the fact that there was no sound at the beginning of the history of cinema. Strong gesticulation and facial expressions itself led to the fact that the acting resembled comedy, and very often the acting resembled circus acts. The tasks of the genre remained the same. They are to induce laughter in the audience. Melodramas, we can say, are designed more for a female audience, as they appeal primarily to the feelings of the viewer. There is the presence of positive heroes, villains and intrigue. An adventure film always has a dynamic plot and keeps the viewer in suspense, and the heroes - always in an extreme situation. Western - is also considered an adventure film, but unlike a simple adventure film, the western was born in America. Western style movies must necessarily be associated with the atmosphere of the Wild West. Detectives are investigative films that solve some kind of crime. The main characters are police detectives or even criminals. In the case of the detective, screen versions of literary works are especially good. The thriller genre keeps the viewer in suspense from the beginning to the end of the film. This genre contains elements of both detective and adventure films. But a peculiarity of this genre is mystery. Gangster movies, in their turn, tell about the organized crime or about the gangsters. Another genre is the catastrophe films that mainly show the large-scale disasters. A distinctive feature of such films is considered to be the involvement of many people, mass scenes. The thriller is a comparatively new genre. It is also considered to be an adventure film with a lot of fight scenes, shooting and chases. The historical genre includes biographical films and historical dramas. These films can be based on real historical events. There are often screen adaptations of literary works. The same applies to fantasy films. But in this case, the work is written by fiction writers. These are films based on unreal, fantastic events. Horror films show unnatural and mystical events. The point of films is to provoke fear and suspense. At all times a master in the art of horror films is considered the director Alfred Hitchcock, who manages to make something scary out of the ordinary and simple (the film "The Birds"). And then there are political films that talk about any political process or ideology. They can also include elements of an action or adventure film, be biographical or investigative, but they are always based on political events. The great Alexander Sergeyevich Pushkin believed that the most unrealistic of genres is the drama genre[23] . If we consider the thought of the great

---

[23] From the course of lectures by R. Hayrapetyan as part of the course "Literary and Aesthetic Criticism as a

writer, we can conclude that the audience does not take seriously those actions that develop in such a short period of time. One man's life, with all its contradictions, is shown in a three-hour movie. And so, since we are talking about the most "unrealistic" genre in fiction film, it is worth noting about the most realistic kind of cinematography. We are talking about a documentary that shows real characters in the real world.

Component of Journalism".

CHAPTER 2. TELEVISION AND DOCUMENTARY FILMMAKING

2.1. Documentary: Varieties and Peculiarities

There are many varieties of documentaries: newsreels, newsreels that are created for history, film fixation (video surveillance, scientific filming), author's journalism and art (film prose, film poetry, film drama, film melodrama, film comedy, film tragedy, etc.). But all the same, it is impossible to exhaust the multitude of documentary genres. First of all, documentary is not only a part of cinematography, but also a mass medium. Even in the law of the Republic of Armenia, the first article states that documentary and documentary filmmaking are media outlets. Author's journalism includes film reportage, film essay, film diary, social film journalism, film investigation, portrait film, and film journey.

Documentary film (non-fiction) may well have elements of fiction. It all depends on the author. He can provoke his characters into different manifestations - anger, joy, admiration. It can also completely expose the personality of the hero. One way or another, documentary film deals with elements of the game - cinema involves play. In English documentary terminology, there is a more precise contrast between fiction and non-fiction, that is, with and without fiction. Godfrey Reggio, the famous American filmmaker, creator of experimental documentaries, was also famous for his famous phrase. A living legend says that in a feature film the director is God, but in a documentary God is the director. Indeed, documentary filmmaking is all about unpredictability. The director does not know before shooting how the course of events will change in the course of shooting. He doesn't know his character until the end. It may happen that the hero himself creates the mood of the film. Something unusual and unpredictable may suddenly happen during the shooting. In that case the cameraman has no right to miss that important moment. Here much depends not only on the director and the hero, but also on the cameraman. Teamwork is important in making a documentary. The same goes for journalism. If a journalist makes a film reportage, a film essay or a film portrait, he must adhere to several rules of documentary filmmaking. First of all, it is very good to know your hero (if you have one), so you can control the situation in any case, since it is considered an author's work after all. Secondly, the author must work together with the cameraman, discuss with him the process of shooting, exchange ideas, be careful not to let the cameraman miss important details. First of all you should have a ready script in your head, present certain shots, but in addition to all that the author should also be able to adapt well to what is going on. Another very important factor in the creation of documentary production is the ability to improvise. It is important not to miss a moment, and to be able to capture it. Maybe completely new ideas and shots will emerge on the set. All of this is not as easy as it seems. There are often opinions that a documentary is easier to make than a feature film. But not everyone can concentrate and adjust so quickly on set. If everything goes according to plan, it's easier to work. A very important role is played by the ability to communicate, to ask questions of characters, to reveal a person's inner world. All this is important not only for the author of the documentary, but also for the journalist-interviewer. A journalist in the creation of a documentary must take into account all these aspects and have a full package of these qualities. The documentary filmmaker must be passionate about the subject and the character. It doesn't matter if he or she is a journalist or not. The journalist should be interested not only in a particular subject, but in absolutely everything. In documentaries he is the participant of the film, the creator of a new work. Not only he must be interested in the subject, but he himself must be interested in the characters. As for the cameraman, he actually plays a huge role. It is he who chooses the right angle and plan, just pushes the button to start shooting. And of course, a separate role is played by an editor. He selects the necessary frames and builds a story line. The final result depends on the cooperation between the director and editor. It turns out that the author - a journalist or director, is the link during the whole process of creating a film. In addition to all this, there are also several criteria that must be kept in mind when creating a documentary. Before you begin the filmmaking process, you need to clearly understand what the film will be about and why it should be of interest to the viewer. By answering these questions, you can send the energy of the film crew in the right direction. The hero of the film should not treat the camera as a terrible mechanism. For him to remain only the cameraman as a person. It is better to have as few people on the set as possible. The hero must get used to the cameras and the people on the set. The director and cameraman must coordinate their actions discreetly and communicate by means of signs, so that the hero pays less attention to the camera and behaves naturally. The most important thing in a documentary is the characters. The camera should not miss a single dialogue with people with his participation, as it is they who very accurately reveal the character of the hero. Covert shooting plays an important role in the documentary. The cameraman can shoot the hero so that the latter does not even notice that the camera is on. He can pretend to turn the camera off and look at the character instead of the viewfinder, or he can turn the camera on and turn it inconspicuously toward the character. It might happen that the best shots are made during covert shooting. The cameraman, just like the director, must think in montage terms. He has to keep in mind the already filmed shots and filter all the material. If he knows his stuff well, he won't need much footage, but the final result will be better. You have to have a basic line that connects all the material.

Documentary film has its origins in the birth of cinema. People may not realize it right away, but when we look at the history of cinema, we see that the very first film shown to an audience on December 28, 1895, by the Lumière brothers was a documentary. We have referred to this picture several times throughout the work. There seemed to be nothing unusual about the arrival of a train at La Ciotat station. But in this film, what was brilliant was life itself, as it were. Ordinary passengers would get off the train and not even realize that the person standing in front of them twirling the knob was, in fact, the cameraman who was filming them. This is where life is unique in its authenticity and uniqueness. That's what documentary filmmaking is all about! Much later, Andrei Tarkovsky would call "Arrival of a Train" a film of genius. It was only later that the masters of documentary filmmaking would begin to realize that this was not only a chronicle of life, but a form of cinema in its own right. Among them, the following phrase will become famous: "Life is more talented than I am"[24] . If we compare documentary filmmakers with the masters of feature films, they do not need to invent plots and individual characters, they do not need actors, makeup or special sets, they do not need to invent dialogues for the actors. Everything is different here. Here the director uses life itself as his material. It is life that offers him special moments capable of astonishing and expressing lofty ideas. The only thing left to do is not to miss those special moments, to see them and capture them in time with the camera. One of the greatest privileges of non-fiction cinema is that it is possible to show the viewer something he or she cannot see themselves: not every ordinary citizen could see the coronation of Nicholas II (narrative by Camille Cerf, 1896), not everyone can afford to go to Niagara Falls, or not everyone can visit Leo Tolstoy at his Yasnaya Polyana mansion (narrative by Alexander Drankov, 1908). This story is considered to be the beginning of Russian cinema, although many amateur pieces had been shot before that. Cinematographers have always been attracted by sensational incidents,

---

[24] Encyclopedia Krugosvet. Documentary Film//.
http://www.krugosvet.ru/enc/kultura i obrazovanie/theatr i kino/DOKUMENTALNOE KINO.html?pag e=0.1

exoticism, natural disasters, technical innovations, car racing - anything that could attract the attention of the viewer. A great many cameramen may even have put their lives in danger to get the footage they want. There is a legend in the history of cinema about a cameraman who shot a lion and spun the handle of the film camera until the lion jumped on him and he still continued to shoot it. For a long time there was no clear line between fiction and documentary filmmaking. Neither filmmakers nor the audience thought about it. In 1902 Méliès in the pavilion of his studio in Montreux shoots a staged version of the coronation of King Edward VII of England, with extras dressed up in matching outfits. He shoots his film on the eve of the real coronation, but it is ahead of the release of the authentic chronicle footage. All the audience watches the film with great confidence, and the king himself even recognizes himself. It took a long time to understand the differences between the two arts. It took a long time for art cinema to assert itself as a separate art form. Only then would documentary film be able to understand its own characteristics and its role in filmmaking.

Robert Flaherty, who was a mining engineer, has his own special contribution to the development of documentary film.

In the 1910s, he was exploring the Canadian Polar region, looking for oil. And one day on one of his trips he took a movie camera with him and shot a lot of scenes about Eskimos. But, unfortunately, Flaherty accidentally set fire to the film with a cigarette while he was gathering material on the editing table. As a result, the entire negative was lost. The next time he took the camera again, but with a specific purpose. In the fall of 1919, he began shooting his famous future film Nanook of the North (1922).[25]

This time the episodes of the film united the image of the main character, an Eskimo, who waged a harsh struggle for life with the nature of the North. The film was an incredible success among the audience. Even during the days of the film, ice cream of the popular "eskimo" variety was sold in the lobby and has survived to this day. This speaks volumes about the popularity of the film. So what was the film's success? In addition to capturing the viewer with the unusual nature of the North, the film showed humanity and love for the main character. The film had its own special philosophy. It was also the first time it showed the representatives of the small people exactly as they saw themselves, not from the side of the colonizers. This film is the first experience of creating a documentary by long observation. In

---

[25] Encyclopedia Krugosvet. Documentary Film. Founders// http://www.krugosvet.ru/enc/kultura i obrazovanie/theatr i kino/DOKUMENTALNOE KINO.html?pag e=0,1

another famous film, Man of Aran, he shows the inhabitants of a small island who finish their food by hunting sharks. The main theme of his films remains the theme of man in the natural world. The director has not even made a dozen films, his last being Louisiana Story. He himself called his last film a "fantasy," and the history of cinema calls the film a nostalgic elegy. Flaherty's paintings were different in that they showed the characters in the ordinary circumstances of life, so they remained natural, there was no artificiality. That was the main principle of the great master's work. Thanks to this style, documentaries are so popular in the West, and in the Soviet documentary film industry it began to develop in the 1960s. In honor of Flaherty, Perm documentary enthusiast Pavel Pechenkin will name the festival of new documentary films "Flahertyana". New works of Russian and foreign documentary filmmakers are shown at the festival. In 2000, for the first time a contest was held, where the main prize was called "Golden Nanook".

Another very famous master of documentary filmmaking, Dziga Vertov, is a Russian classic who left a huge legacy. He is one of the founders of documentary filmmaking as one of the main directions of cinematographic art. The director's real name is Denis Arkadievich Kaufman. He began his career by working at the newsreel department of the Moscow Film Committee, took part in the editing work of the first Soviet newsreel Kinonedelya, and during the Civil War directed shootings at the front (Fight at Tsaritsyn, Agitpropozdok VTSIK, The Story of the Civil War). Dziga Vertov creates a group of innovative documentary filmmakers. The group was formulated in 1919 and was called "Kinoki." He thought that the documentary screen should not copy the human vision. That's what the "Kino-eye" is for, which is more perfect than ordinary vision. Dziga Vertov was a follower of new ways of filmmaking, new methods of shooting, new, modern subjects on the screen. He loved to experiment, and these experiments brought a lot of new things to chronicle-documentary cinematography. But on the other hand, they caused an ideological vagueness of the idea and complexity of the language. All of this impeded the viewer's perception of the picture. With all this, Vertov wanted to show people something that was difficult to see with the ordinary human eye. He tried to show many processes in life that were hidden from the human eye with the help of various technical possibilities of the camera. With the subsequent editing of the material, he could clearly explore reality. He wanted to explore the world with the cinematic eye. He firmly believed that a filmmaker should show real events from life, not fiction that is created for a specific purpose. In his articles "Kinoki," "We," "The Coup," "He," and "The Cinema

Eye," he even denied the artist the right to fiction, arguing that the artist must document reality, that is, capture, immortalize it. Very often these pioneering thoughts were condemned by film critics. Behind his bold challenges they did not notice his advanced ideas. On his initiative the production of a new thematic newsreel "Kinopravda" began, each issue of which had its own clear artistic solution. It was during this period that he carries out his new creative experiment - a film "Kino-Eye", which won a prize at the International Exhibition in Paris. The film was otherwise known as "Life in the Eye." The film is about a man in a documentary-poetic non-staged film.

In the second half of the 1920s, Dziga Vertov continued to develop his theories, researching the importance of intervals between movements for montage.

He himself writes that working on the film "The Man with the Camera" required more tension than previous film-eye work. This was because of the greater number of points under observation and the complex organizational and technical filming operations. The film was at the very center of life. The camera in it becomes the main participant in life.[26]

In the fall of 1964, during a survey at the thirteenth Mannheim International Film Festival, film critics from 24 countries named The Man with the Camera as one of the 20 best documentaries of all time. Vertov brought a completely new language to filmmaking: the camera was no longer just filming from the sidelines, but became a direct participant in all the action of the film. The same thing is seen today in most journalistic reporting. Just as then the picture "Man with a Movie Camera" represented an attack by movie cameras on reality, so now the "journalist" with a camera and microphone in his hands penetrates every sphere of life. One could say that Vertov, together with his group of "kino-people," created the foundations for the future of television reporting.

Among the groundbreaking works created by Vertov are also "The Sixth Part of the World," "Symphony of the Donbass," "Three Songs about Lenin," and "Lullaby. With the advent of sound in cinema, Vertov makes another discovery - along with industrial noises in his film "Symphony of the Donbass," he also records the workers' remarks. Three years later, Vertov shoots his first interview in a documentary with one of the heroines of the Dneproges. After this interview, the group not only recorded authentic sounds and noises, it also carried out a series of synchronous filming, that is, it combined the image with sound recording. Vertov strove for his films not to be dubbed, but at once sound. It was this film by Vertov that

---

[26]   Dziga V. Articles, Diaries, Concepts. Moscow: Art. 1966. C. 160

marked the beginning of the chronicle sounds that were organized into a symphony. With the end of World War II, he returned from evacuation in 1944 and made his last film, The Oath of Youth. After that he began directing the work of front-line cameramen. In the mature period of his creative work Vertov developed his individual style of montage. Montage gradually becomes a way of expressing the emerging real art of documentary filmmaking. It was also used by S. Eisenstein and A. Dovzhenko. One of his most important achievements is a theoretical, montage concept of documentary cinema. Vertov believed that montage was not just a way of organizing movement, but the most important element of the specifics of cinema. He also talked about the fundamental differences between the montage of feature and documentary films. Editing a documentary begins long before the director picks up the pieces of film already filmed. The material is edited from the moment the subject is chosen until the film is released on the screen. Footage is edited throughout the filmmaking process.

Vertov always said that art should serve to promote revolutionary ideas[27] . He became a true classic of documentary filmmaking through his creative and theoretical research. He laid the foundations of a new artistic-documentary genre of cinema and played a great role in the development of Soviet and foreign documentary cinematography. He also made a profound study of the human soul and psychology, which led him to the search for methods to influence the mass audience. Vertov's work was deeply ideological. In his manifestos and in his directorial practice he did not consider the ordinary fixation of reality to be a phenomenon of art; on the contrary, he believed that art requires a figurative interpretation of reality, emotional excitement, and an ideological orientation, with the ideas of revolution in mind. A small part from Vertov's manifesto We:

"WE call ourselves cinephiles, unlike the 'cinephiles,' a herd of junkers who are good at peddling their own rags. WE see no connection between the guile and calculation of the peddlers and true cinematography. WE declare old films, romantic, theatrical, etc. - leprosy. WE temporarily dismiss the human being as an object of filmmaking because of his inability to control his own movements. Cinematography is the art of organizing the necessary movements of things in space and time into a rhythmic artistic whole, in harmony with the properties of the material and the inner rhythm of each thing.[28]

The cinephiles advocated a new man who was free from weightiness and clumsiness,

---

[27]   Dziga Vertov//UeTsou.gi// http://www.vertov.ru/Dziga_Vertov
[28]   Vertov D. We//Theatre//#8, 2012//http://oteatre.info/my-variant-manifesta/

who could direct his own movements. They advocated dynamism in the art of cinema, movement and the search for the cinematic gamma. They also believed that cinema was the art of fictionalizing the movements of things in space, and advocated the realization of the unrealizable in life by cinematography. Their ideas were fresh, new and daring.

One of the most interesting attempts in cinematography made by Vertov was the film Cinema Eye. It was the first attempt in the world to create a film without actors, directors, without using sets, costumes[29] . All the acting people in the film continue to do what they normally do. The picture presents an attack by cinematic apparatuses on reality and prepares the theme of all-creating labor. The cinematic apparatus gives each worker the opportunity to see for himself that things are made by him, they belong to him. They enable them to see the truth and question the need to clothe and feed a society of parasites (the Flirtatious Bourgeois, the fat-filled bourgeois).

Vertov and his group of filmmakers believed that cinema was and is on the wrong track. Yesterday's and today's cinema is a commercial affair. Each picture is only a literary skeleton wrapped in a film skin. At best, under this skin we see the fat and the meat of the film, but we don't see the main thing, the backbone of the film. The path of cinematic development has been dictated by considerations of profit. There is nothing strange about the fact that the big trade in films - illustrations of novels, Pinkerton releases - blinded [29] the eyes of the producers.[30]

Vertov and Flaherty are considered as antipodes, ideologists of two different directions of documentary filmmaking. Flaherty always followed the truth of life, while Vertov constructed life in favor of the propaganda idea.

In the late 1920s, previously filmed documentary footage is interpreted differently and becomes a strong ideological tool. The filmmaker Esther Schoub deserves great credit for this. The woman filmmaker marked the beginning of the development of the historical-documentary method in cinema. She is the author of "The Fall of the Romanov Dynasty," "Leo Tolstoy" and "Russia of Nicholas II. Through her pictures the director led the viewer to conclusions about the antagonism of classes and the justice of the revolutionary upheaval. Esfir Shub created a series of montage films on the basis of her reinterpretation of chronicle film material. As a result of her many experiments she proved the possibility of a purely emotional impact of the old chronicle.

---

[29]   Dziga V. Articles, Diaries, Concepts. Moscow: Art. 1966. C. 68
[30] Dziga V. Articles, Diaries, Concepts. Moscow: Art. 1966. C. 70

The English filmmaker John Grierson (1989-1972) had his great influence on the development of world documentary filmmaking. Because he was a sociologist, he saw documentary film as a new kind of journalism, a means of propaganda and of influencing society. Grierson brought documentary filmmaking back from the exotic edges to what is under our noses. His film, Fishermen's Vessels, showed the daily life of British fishermen. It was a real revolutionary discovery, as it was the first time people saw man in the process of labor.

Grierson insisted that the making of a new film required a binding "ironclad script" where all the details of future shoots would be precisely stipulated. Robert Flaherty, on the contrary, believed that the script should give freedom to the documentary. He suggested that a documentary's script should be written by life itself.

And indeed, when we study the principles of the various masters of documentary filmmaking, we have repeatedly found that documentary filmmaking is always unpredictable. Here we can also recall Godfrey Reggio's aforementioned famous words about the difference between fiction and non-fiction. On the set, reality can change all the director's previous plans. All this was confirmed in Flaherty's script for Industrial Britain (1932), which he directed with his antipode Grirson. There was only one phrase in the script, that the film would consist of pictures of industrial Britain. But in the script controversy Vertov was more decisive when in the credits of his famous film The Man with the Camera he stated that the film was unscripted.

A separate role in the development of philosophical-poetic cinema is played by the work of American director Godfrey Reggio, whose famous words we have repeatedly mentioned above. The author of experimental documentaries is also known for his film trilogy "Katsi: "Koyanisqatsi," "Povakkatsi," and "Nakoykatsi." He spent several years making his Koyanisqatsi, which was released in 1983. The title of the film, in the language of the Gopi Indians, means "life that has lost its equilibrium." It looks, as if with indifferent eyes, at the bustle of big cities, at the smoke of the atmosphere and at the pollution of our environment, in the end, at humanity, which is ruined by technological progress. A continuation of the same ideas of the director is the film Povakkatsi (1988), which means "life in transformation. In the film, the director wanted to show how modern civilization can affect developing countries. To make the film, Reggio traveled to 12 countries: Egypt, India, Peru, Brazil, Nigeria, Kenya, Nepal. Nakoykatsi's latest film is "life as war" (2003). The film is about a war where everyone is fighting over the possession of technology. Nature is oppressed by the latest technology. Compared to his previous films, the director doesn't use a lot of nature footage in this one. Instead, he shows mixed images of the modern world that are digitally processed. According to the director, he uses the "image as scene" method. This is the method by which he creates an image of global reality. The director used in his films the mesmerizing music of composer Philip Glass, which was inseparable from the image. The director's latest masterpiece was The Visitors, which he made in 2013. There's no telling what exactly this film is about. It definitely doesn't have one clear idea. It acts more on the emotions and perception of a person.

"My film is a kind of perception test. If 10 people watch a film, soon five of them leave because they were looking for meaning and didn't find it, or they just got bored. But those who stay have very different experiences. The film doesn't give people a clear explanation, it gives people an opportunity to 30
to see something unique.[31]

As the author says, his films are journeys we plan ourselves, compared to Hollywood entertainment films. Godfrey Reggio is a contemporary of ours who had no directorial training, he worked with troubled teens and bullies and mentored them on the right path. One day he showed his charges the film "The Forgotten" directed by Luis Buñuel, which made a strong impression on the children and on the director himself. In this way he found a tool for himself to influence people. He began to make his brilliant films, through which he sent people not one general meaning for all, but for each individual.

Documentary film was also strongly influenced by the work of Eisenstein. Some researchers, such as Paul Roth, also consider him a documentary filmmaker. And his masterpiece The Battleship Potemkin was long considered a masterpiece of Soviet documentary cinema in catalogs. Eisenstein's films chronicled true events. They had no protagonist or storyline. Frames from the film were repeatedly used by editors as an authentic chronicle. Well, documentary filmmakers often recreate events of the past, while using real characters and actors. And the ethics of documentary filmmaking is that it always stays true to the truth. Eisenstein served precisely this purpose and answered those who classified his films as documentaries very clearly: "The film acts like a drama, but is built like a

---

[31] Laifurov. A. Words mean nothing more//Interview//01.07.2014,15:34//
http://www.interviewrussia.ru/movie/godfri-redzhio-slova-bolshe-nichego-ne-znachat?page=7

chronicle."[32]

Eisenstein's work strongly influenced many documentary filmmakers. One such master is Walter Ruttman (18871941), who was a poster painter, creator of one of the first abstract films, and a serious student of architecture and music. "Berlin: Symphony of the Big City (Berlin - Die Sinfonie der GroBstadt,1927) is his most famous film, which also has the influence of Vertov. The film is constructed as a musical canvas consisting of many episodes of metropolitan life: nameless people with their cares rushing to work, street traffic, the bustle of the business day, spinning machine parts, dancing cabaret dancers, newspaper boys. The millions of human faces in the frame are reduced to each other and quite what is moving by, hurrying or resting. Berlin becomes the film's only protagonist. The film is not accompanied by a soundtrack, although the very title of the film suggests the possibility of a musical reading of it. The montage conveys the hectic rhythm of the city's life and offers a particularly dynamic narrative style. Here we found similarities of some shots with the famous shots from Lumière's pictures "Arrival of a Train" and "Exit from the Factory", when people get off the train or from the factory, and the flow of people moves in the same direction. The film was accompanied by live music by Dmitri Shubin.

Karl Mayer wrote the screenplay for the picture. One day, standing amidst the impending traffic at Zoological Park, the screenwriter suddenly conceived his Symphony of the City. Art historian Paul Rota wrote that the artificiality and all sorts of constraints of working in the pavilion bored Meyer. His earlier films had been made in the studio. He lost interest in fiction and wanted his subjects to grow out of reality. The film Berlin: Symphony of the Big City becomes a textbook of documentary filmmaking.[33]

Similar urban symphonies were produced afterwards, although before Berlin was created, director Alberto Cavalcanti produced Only Time (1926), a film about Paris. The film showed a day in the life of Parisian workers and also sought social generalizations. This was also the case with M. Kaufman's Moscow: One Day in the Life of the City (1927). The director was inspired by the stunning texture and nature of Moscow and showed life in a city still untouched by grandiose reconstruction.

The abstract perception asserts that the director focuses on montage rhythms, which

---

[32] Eisenstein in Memoirs of Contemporaries. Moscow: Art. 1974. C. 252

[33] Encyclopedia Krugosvet. Documentary Film. Founders// http://www.krugosvet.ru/enc/kultura i obrazovanie/theatr i kino/DOKUMENTALNOE KINO.html?pag e=0,1

leads to a further departure from reality to the abstract. This is evidenced, characteristic of avant-garde films, by the presence of frames of altered reality. Thus, real objects are filmed in such a way that they are transformed into abstract drawings.

Among the discoveries of the masters of the 1920s are poetic documentaries. Such were the films "Rain" (1928) and "The Bridge" (1929) by the Dutch director Joris Ivens (1898-1989). For four months he filmed Amsterdam in the rain. He filmed the streets, the river, streetcars, cars, roofs and windows of houses, passers-by with umbrellas, and put all these shots into a harmonious musical and poetic sequence. Ivens's films are close to the aesthetics of French avant-garde films. Then the director began making pictures with more acute social problems: "Song of Heroes", "Borinage", about the miners' strike in Belgium, "Four hundred million", about Japanese aggression in China, "Our Russian Front", also about the war with fascism, etc. A special place in the work of the director takes poetic film "Seine meets Paris" (1957). The film gives the impression that the river Seine stands still and Paris is flowing past it. In the film, poetry is inherent in every frame, in the actions of all the characters. Every frame is poetic. The shots are accompanied by a reading of Jacques Prévert's poems behind the scenes, and the expressive editing gives the film a special shape.

In the years of sound cinema other films appeared accompanied by poetic texts. One striking example of such films was Night Mail (1936) directed by Basil Wright and Harry Watt, who were also followers of Grirson, the producer of Night Mail. The authors of the tape created an accurate story, filled with poetry, about a crew of the Night Express carrying mail to Scotland. The film features poetry by Whisten Hugh Auden and music by Benjamin Britten.

In the socially oriented documentaries of the early 1930s, an important and decisive experience was the "film train" of Alexander Medvedkin, who was always faithful to the ideas of the revolution. The director considered it necessary for cinema to intervene in life in order to propagandize and build socialism. What were the specifics of the work of the "film train"? A specially equipped train carriages housed a film laboratory, a projection unit, and a print shop. Documentary filmmakers would set off on the roads of the country, arrive at construction sites or production facilities and make films about the problems that arose in the process of working collectives. Then a film crew on the spot developed, processed the material, edited it, provided subtitles and organized screenings with the characters, followed by a lively discussion of the plot. The travelling film studio operated from 1932 to 1934 and made twelve trips. Under the influence of the group's activities in the 1960's in many countries created the same groups and develops "alternative cinema". In France a "Medvedkin group" was created, with Chris Marker as its leader. He would later dedicate the film "Medvedkin's Tomb" to Medvedkin.

Among the propaganda documentaries was Triumph of the Will (1935) directed by Leni Riefenstahl. The film, about the VI Congress of the German National Socialist Party in Nuremberg, included the meeting of Hitler descending on an airplane, his passing among the crowds, the grand parade, and the night torchlight procession. But the main point of the film was to unite the nation around the leader of the country. The film is a hymn to the glory of Hitler. Twenty-six cameramen worked on the film, and the film reformer was able to include new technical means: panoramas from a specially built elevator, from roller skates, from a cart moving on rails. She edited the footage for six months. She spent 18 hours a day in the editing room. The result of this tremendous work was a talented director's film. Leni's next film was more perfect in its technical and artistic means and larger than the previous one. The two-part "Olympia" (1936-1938), which lasted 200 minutes, with the anonymous director Walter Ruttman. The first series is "The Feast of Nations," and the second series is "The Feast of Beauty." The film poem is about the 1936 Olympic Games in Berlin. It glorified the beauty of the human body, the strength of the athletes' spirit and their will to win. In 1940, Leni shoots the film "German Armor", which glorified the attack of German tanks on Paris.

And so, the most important theme for filmmakers becomes the fight against fascism. It is during this period that Ivens makes his film about the Spanish Civil War, "Spanish Land". Ernest Hemingway writes the text for the film. At this time many cameramen, both feature and non-feature, find themselves on the fronts of the Great Patriotic War. S. Shkolnikov, who was also among these cameramen and directors, later recalled that there were 252 of them, but one in five died in the battles, and if they remained alive, they were wounded or shell-shocked. He recalled that three and a half million meters of film in those 1,418 days of the war were "worth its weight in blood," and now this film is worth its weight in gold. It was very important for documentary filmmakers that in those years feature filmmakers also turned to the war theme. Alexander Dovzhenko together with Yu. Solntseva and Ya. Avdeenko in 1943 filmed "The Battle for Our Soviet Ukraine" and "Victory on the Right-Bank Ukraine" with Yu. Such films enriched documentary cinema with interesting artistic solutions and authorship.

During World War II, Frank Capra, the master of feature films, became famous in America for his social comedies. The director was commissioned by the Pentagon to make a series of propaganda films. General George Marshall then appointed him to lead a group that included such directors as John Ford, John Huston, and Louis Milestone. The group produced a series of montage films, collectively titled "Why Are We at War?" that fought fascism. Capra created his own film, included in the series, The Battle for Russia.

The documentary filmmakers of England, who have always played a huge role in the development of world documentary filmmaking, also opposed fascism. During the war years Humphrey Jennings became a famous figure, who created the films "London Will Endure This", "Listen to Britain", "The Fires Have Started", "Diary for Timothy", etc. In his films he showed a country at war: ordinary people - musicians, housewives, radio announcers, firefighters who did their duty, despite the war, continued life and went about their usual business. It was these kinds of tapes that raised the spirit of the nation.

2.2. Varieties and Features of Armenian Cinematography

Documentary cinema in Armenia was born in 1924, but before that there were some materials that showed the Armenian life and life of the people. One such material, made in 1910, was the funeral of Catholicos Matteos Izmirlian in Echmiadzin. The first serious Armenian documentary was "Khorurdayin Hayastan". The script was written by E. Chubar, D. Dznuni and P. Folyan, and the film was shot by a group of cameramen of the State Photo Cinema of Armenia. The editing was supervised by I. Kraslavski. The film was screened on the occasion of the fourth anniversary of the establishment of the Soviet regime in Armenia. The picture was not only a chronicle of reality, but also interpreted it in an artistic and imaginative way.

The first documentaries did not yet have a director, there was only camerawork, but in 1926 Amo Bek-Nazaryan appears, filming the consequences of a strong earthquake in Leninakan. In 1930 the director shoots a documentary film "Country-Nairi", in which he uses both documentary filming and fragments of fiction, staging with actors, striving to depict reality figuratively.

Armenian documentary filmmakers also did a lot during the Great Patriotic War. Frontline cameramen (V. Haykazyan, I. Dildarian, G.
Sanamian) filmed the actions of Armenian military groups in Kerch. During that period 54

issues of the newsreel "Soviet Armenia" were released as well as seven documentaries. It is no coincidence that the first Armenian feature (silent) film was "Namus" (1926) by Bek-Nazarov.[34]

It was decided to film the famous novel of the same name by Alexander Shirvanzade. At that time, there were excellent Armenian theatrical actors (Racia Nersesyan, Avet Avetian, Hovhannes Abelyan, Maria Shakhubanyan-Tatieva, Tatiana Hakobyan, etc.), who created beautiful images in the film. Shirvanzadeh's "Namus" suited BekNazarov's creative predilections as much as possible. On the one hand, he saw in the play a deeply realistic portrayal of reality, on the other hand - a romantic love story of two young people. It had a truthful description of life in a provincial Armenian town, psychological portraits of its inhabitants, as well as an attractive melodramatic plot that ends with the death of lovers. It was through all this that "Namus" was to appeal to Bek-Nazarov. His approach to cinema was not homogeneous: "Orientalism", adherence to adventure-romantic plots in the works of the director combined with realistic tendencies, with an intuitive striving for the truth of life. Beck-Nazarov himself wrote:

"At the time, I didn't yet have a conscious desire to break away from exotic oriental film."[35]

The film showed the all-powerful power of an age-old custom, the invincibility of "adat", and people's slavish dependence on it. The main characters of the film, Seyran and Susan, motivated by mutual love, disregarded the grandfather's custom and did not obey the concepts of "Namus", and therefore perished. The heroine dies at the hands of her husband, blinded by jealousy, and the hero then commits suicide. But this situation is only outwardly melodramatic. In fact, the writer wanted to show a sharpened thought about the viciousness and unnaturalness of patriarchal and mestizo notions of honor and the human tragedies they generate. This was a winning dramatic subject for Bek-Nazarov. The artist's intuition told the director that only staying true to the realistic spirit of the work of the Armenian classic, he would be able to create a film free of falsehood, a film that is close and necessary for people[35].

The last Armenian silent film was "Gikor" and the first sound film "Pepo" was released in 1935. One of the most significant films in Armenian documentary filmmaking was

---

[34]   Kalantar K. L. Amo Bek-nazarov. E.: "Hayastan", 1973. p. 19-22
[35]   Kalantar K. L. Amo Bek-nazarov. E.: "Ayastan", 1973. p. 20

"Motherland", which was released in 1946. The art director and author of the narrator was the famous Soviet film director A. Dovzhenko. The film told about the Armenian people in the pre-October and post-October periods. In his text Dovzhenko tells that half of the Armenian people were tortured and crucified by yatagans and now the bones of the martyrs are whitewashed behind the Turkish border. It is far from the past, he says. Garib's song "Goodbye, Armenia!" was also heard in the text. In the years that followed, this film played a huge role in the mass repatriation of Armenians.

In the 1950s, significant new documentaries appeared in Armenia, including "Echmiadzin Armenian Church Cathedral", "Waters of Sevan", "Armenia Today", "Egishe Charents", "Native Song", etc. The film "Pink City" directed by G. Balasanyan is also worth mentioning. In the film the old Yerevan with its neglected houses and streets is contrasted with the new reconstructed Yerevan with its beautiful architecture and blossoming streets.

In the 1960s, along with talented directors of the older generation (G. Balasanyan, L. Isahakyan, V. Haykazyan, R. Frangulyan, etc.) there were also such younger directors as R. Gevorkyants, A. Vauni, A. Peleshyan. A. Shahbazyan, P. Malayan. Through documentaries filmmakers tried to show construction sites, industrial enterprises, all the wealth of fields. They told about the great cultural figures, contemporary writers, artists, military leaders and revolutionaries. There were also films about Matenadaran, where ancient Armenian manuscripts are kept, about different tourist routes in Armenia, about a zoo. All the films showed the blossoming Armenia and the prosperity of the country.

The films of Armenian documentary filmmakers were shown on all-Union and foreign screens and made their great contribution to the history of world documentary filmmaking. It was during these years that films-portraits of many Armenian writers, publicists, artists, pilots, scientists, musicians, actors and directors were created: "Sero Khanzadyan", "Stepan Zoryan", "The Green Poplar of Nairi".

In 1965 a popular science film "Byurakan Observatory" was released, which presented the essence of the doctrine of stellar worlds by the famous academician Victor Hambardzumyan. The most important film of the 1960s was "Martiros Saryan", directed by L. Vagharshyan and shot by M. Varzhapetyan. The narrator's text was written by Ilya Ehrenburg and the music by the artist's son Lazar Saryan.

In 1977 the "Yerevan Film Studio of Chronic and Documentary Films" was renamed into the "Armenian Documentary Film Studio". The main themes of that period were the heroic work of the Soviet people, the strengthening of friendship between peoples, the formation of communist ideas, the problems of economic life, ways of improving the economy, industry, agriculture, etc.

Director Artavazd Peleshian has made a special and unparalleled contribution to Armenian documentary filmmaking. His worldview, individual cinematographic outlook, artistic style, and profound understanding of the role of montage in cinema make his understanding of the people, time and the human being relevant and naked. In his films the line between fiction and non-fiction is blurred. They surprise with their energy and montage, to which he himself gave the term "distant" in his films. He discovered a generalized portrait of the Armenian nation, gave a precisely contemporary image of the Armenian people: his films had no specific hero and no commentary. Pleshian spoke of the people, the humanity, the country. The strong spirit of the Armenian people is expressed in his films "We", "The Seasons". He uses his theory of remote editing in such films as "The Land of Men," "Night Patrol," "The Beginning," and "The Inhabitants.

"It's dark... To the disturbing sound of orchestral music, the face of a little girl with disheveled hair appears frozen out of the darkness. She looks ahead with a mournful look and then slowly disappears again into the darkness.[36]

With the above-mentioned words begins the script of the film "We". Artavazd Peleshyan remains steadfastly faithful to cinema even outside of it. The scripts of his films are strictly epigraphic, but in them the director's word turns into a means that emphasizes the authentic concreteness of the subject, of the phenomenon. In this way, he brings cinema into the world of the reader's perceptions.

In 1984, Haroutyun Khachatryan came to documentary filmmaking, who managed to make his own special contribution to the development of Armenian documentary cinema. In the director's work it is difficult to determine which type of cinema he favors more - documentary or fiction, due to the fact that he brings a completely new language to cinema and wittily combines non-fiction and fiction in it. His famous films are "Return to the Promised Land," "The Wind of Oblivion," and "The Last Station - Araratian." The director's film "The Poet's Return" was awarded as the best film at the Rotterdam film festival in 2006. Critics have called Khachaturian's film an unrepeatable example of cinematic thinking and cinematic language. After this film the director has received more than 20 invitations to

---

[36] Peleshyan A. My Cinema. E.: "Sovetkan Groh", 1988. p. 23

participate in various international festivals and competitions. Recently the director finished working on his new film from the series "Endless Escape, Everlasting Return" and talked about his film "The Wind of Oblivion" made 25 years ago. That film was also about people who left Armenia for various political, social reasons, in search of daily bread. The director says he has always been interested in why people leave. As a result of the filmmaker's research into different such situations, stories, and types of people, this series came about. He's been filming these people for 25 years. Every six or seven years, he begins to find his characters anew. One of them is a simple artist, another is a self-taught theater director, and the third is an auto mechanic.

"Every person, every fate is one movie. I don't think there is anyone who hasn't wondered why people leave Armenia and why they return. Is it a national character or is it due to circumstances? My desire is not to emphasize the form of this escape, but to give reasons to think seriously about this question."[37]

The director notes that there are also very interesting conversations in the film with a special Armenian flavor that would lose their flavor and aroma if translated. Since 2004, Harutyun Khachatryan has founded and directed the Golden Apricot International Film Festival, which is a great opportunity to promote Armenian culture and national films on the international film scene.

At the 2007 festival, Vardan Hovhannisyan's documentary film "People's Stories of War and Peace" received the most prizes, as well as 20 prizes at international festivals, and was translated into more than 15 languages. The film is about the Karabakh war. It was created in cooperation with BBC, PBS, ARTE (France), WDR (Germany), YLE (Finland) at Bars Media Studio. It consists of two parts: the first part contains documentary shots made during the military actions in Akob Kamar in 1994, the second part shows the life stories of people after the war who were the heroes of the first part of the film. According to the director, the heroes of the film have no hatred, because it is impossible to win with hatred. The main force that kept these people in the trenches was boundless love, love for their land.

"I myself wanted to understand why we went to war of our own free will, because no one wanted to die. One day my seven-year-old son asked me if I was a soldier, and I couldn't find an answer.[38]

---

[37]   Hakobyan G. Harutyun Khachatryan: No one is not interested in why people run away and come back/Aravot//05.04.2013, 11:43 //http://ru.aravot.am/2013/04/05/154609/

[38]   The film "Stories of Men in War and Peace" will be released in Armenia on May 12// News-

We should also mention the large number of documentaries about one of the most tragic pages in the history of the Armenian people - the Armenian Genocide of 1915. Such films are "Armin Wegner: Photographer of Genocide" by director Tigran Khzmalyan, "Return" by French director of Armenian origin Serge Avetikyan, as well as the films "Armenians, Forgive Us!", "Grandsons' Answer" and "Cross in the Crescent Country" by famous TV presenter, journalist Artem Yerkanyan, "Ordinary Genocide" documentary project and others.

Another film worth mentioning is Ruben Gevokyants and Vahe Gevorkyants' "Autumn of the Magician," which was filmed in 2008 and won the main prize at the festival "New Films of the 21st Century," was also awarded the prize "Golden Laurel" and the prize of the President of Armenia. This film is not just about the famous Italian screenwriter, playwright, poet and sculptor Tonino Guerra, but it is also a kind of attempt to look at Armenians in a new way.

Armenian documentary filmmakers such as Frunze Dovlatyan, Genrikh Malyan, Dmitry Kesayants, Stepan Kevorkov, Mikhail Vartanov, Marat Varzhapetyan, and Ara Vauni also developed Armenian documentary cinema. Armenian filmmakers, such as Haroutyun Khachatryan and Vardan Hovhannisyan, put people in the center of attention in their films. Real human stories have become timeless themes. The topic of the human being is still a leading one in most of the journalistic reports, essays, portrait films, etc.

2.3 History of Television Documentary

Russian director Mikhail Romm's film Ordinary Fascism (1965) has a special place in a number of postwar anti-fascist films. In the film the director touches on Hitler's fascism and totalitarianism. The director abandoned the narration; he speaks to the audience on his own behalf, sharing his reflections, pain, and experience with them. His voice, intonation and free and relaxed conversational style of narration gave the film a special meaning. Mikhail Romm boldly and openly expressed his innovative thoughts and through this film he introduced his individual handwriting to cinema. Even back then he was distinguished by his subjective and brilliant speeches, which were always the subject of vigorous public discussion. He could be compared to Dziga Vertov, who was also a courageous revolutionary in the literal and figurative sense of the word. We have already stressed that in his manifestos

Armenia// 11.05.2011,14:32//http://newsarmenia.am/news/culture/culture-20110511- 42451347/

he repeatedly insisted that art should have an ideological orientation. There was complete sincerity in the words of Dziga Vertov and Mikhail Romm. Isn't this the mission of a journalist on television today: not only to inform, but also to sincerely share his thoughts with the broad public? Unfortunately, the image of the individual journalist is often lost in modern television. Many advocate that a journalist should always be neutral and objective in his or her statements. However, can a journalist (especially a television journalist, for whom their own image is very important) be formed as a professional if they do not have their own subjective view of various phenomena? Does he not lose his identity in the general flow of information today? The activities of professionals such as Vladimir Posner and Vladimir Soloviev can provide answers to these questions. Vladimir Posner is now considered one of the best journalists in the world. He has written numerous books, his thoughts are an authority for the vast majority, and, most importantly, he has managed to bring his individual handwriting to modern television journalism. The fact that on Channel One he hosts an authorial program called "Posner" already says a lot about his individual creativity. In addition, Vladimir Posner also likes to open up to the reader in his books. He devoted one of the chapters of his book "Farewell to Illusions" to his reminiscences about Armenians[39] . How sincerely he tells about the remote little house in Sevan, where an Armenian family welcomed him at their table at 2 a.m. and served him food! How he was amazed at the traditions and culture of the Armenian family, perplexed that if the woman of the family does not sit next to them at the table, it does not mean she has no right to speak! On the contrary, the man of an Armenian family listens to the woman and does everything with her permission. It is through such simple storytelling that Vladimir Pozner manages to create a kind of sincere dialogue with the Armenian people[40]

.

When the Cold War broke out, the interests of documentary filmmakers changed. There was little interest in human life and feelings at that time. The reason for this was not only strict censorship requirements, but also the limited possibilities of technology. Such circumstances did not allow documentary filmmakers to create a full-fledged image of a real person. But from the mid-1950s and in the 1960s especially increased interest in

---

[39] Posner V. V. Farewell to Illusions, 2015.// http://www.litres.ru/vladimir-pozner/proschanie- s-illuziyami/chitat-onlayn/

40 Posner about Armenians: They are already older at birth than I will be at the hour of my death///Au8Og//15.17.03,15:24// http://www.aysor.am/ru/news/2013/07/15/vladimir-pozner-about-armenians/641638

documentaries. It was at this time she tried to penetrate the social life of people and show their characters. Soon, the Soviet cinema is observed to address the person through the long observation of his behavior in the usual state of the covert and synchronous shooting. The same method then proved very effective for television. An example of this is the documentary "series" "Control for Adults" by Igor Shadhan.

With the advent of television, the situation in documentary filmmaking changed. It began to finance the development of the necessary techniques and also brought in new genre pursuits. In the late 1950s Robert Drew received a grant to develop new methods of journalism and created the Drew-Associate group in New York. The group developed a technique based on the 16mm format, which had previously been considered amateurish. The technique consisted of silent cameras, portable tape recorders, and ways to synchronize this equipment. With this new technique they made a new film "Primary Election". The film opened a new stage of the screen documentaries. The film was about the two candidates of the Democratic Party. It is about John F. Kennedy and Rubert Humphrey, who fought for the right to represent the party in the presidential election. The film showed meetings, polling stations, recorded the speech of the candidates and the reactions of the listeners. But the camera itself did not interfere with the events, there were no author's comments and direct statements of the heroes, as it was a condition of their consent to be filmed.

Flaherty cameraman Richard Leacock's camera showed Kennedy getting out of the car, walking down the corridor, making his way through the crowd, shaking hands with people, smiling, climbing to the podium, looking around the applauding audience and beginning his speech. It was all filmed in one shot, without the use of editing. It was a rare, new and sincere way of film narration. Shocked by the film, documentary filmmaker Paul Rotha said:

"You've done what we've dreamed of for 30 years, but were unable to do."[41]

The cameraman Leacock perfected the camera so that reporters could be interviewed under any circumstances. And he himself said that they founded a school with very strict canons, determined that a cameraman and a working microphone were enough to make each film. But the latter is no longer a sound engineer, but specifically a journalist.

"We refused to be interviewed at all. But now, when we see a reporter forcing another unfortunate person to swallow a microphone, we think: Oh, my God, what have we done?

---

[41]   Encyclopedia Krugosvet. Documentary Film. Man on Screen// http://www.krugosvet.ru/enc/kultura i obrazovanie/theatr i kino/DOKUMENTALNOE KINO.html?pag e=0

People followed in our footsteps, but their exertions were on such a low cultural level that we professionals realized: we are 42

created a monster."[42]

What Leacock meant was that if you're making a film about a particular person, the most primitive thing you can think of is to ask them a question. They didn't believe a word the person in front of the camera said. It is much more correct to observe the person at work, but this method already requires a lot of time and patience, which television does not like. The director came to the conclusion that the only way to reflect life was to observe it.

The new method in America called the method of "direct cinema", which opened the possibility of creating a film-drama from the material of life itself. Such was the film director Leacock's Eddie Sachs of Indianapolis (1961). For two years he watched as a car racer Eddie Sachs prepares to compete, and each time he loses them, coming in second. Under the terms of the races, the first got everything and the second got nothing. And from the final credits, the viewer learned that the hero died in the next races, hitting a car that had flashed ahead.

Leacock could be called a filmmaker because that's what documentary filmmakers called themselves, who were involved in both writing, directing, and shooting the film.

In France, documentary filmmaker Jean Rouch and philosopher Edgar Morin made an interesting experience. They made a film called "Chronicle of One Summer" (1961). The essence of the film was that they stopped passersby in the streets of Paris and asked if they were happy. The answers of all these people together constituted the image of the time experienced by the country. Rouch himself called the new method "kinopravda," using the title of Vertov's releases. A little later in 1968, Russian TV director Nikita Khubov and cameraman Marina Goldovskaya filmed Weaver, which told the story of the workers of a weaving factory in the town of Furmanovo. It was banned while still in the process of editing. According to Goldovskaya, she realized that a person can be naked in front of the camera to an extent to which the previous documentary film is not even conceived. All these methods were samples to get closer to the person.

Marina Goldovskaya tells us that she was already working at MSU, teaching at the journalism department, and asked one of her brightest and most outstanding students, Alla Zaitseva, to go to this factory and get a job. She began working there and lived with these girls in the dormitory. Goldovskaya went there after two or three months. She also had a

---

[42]   Ibid.

woman, Zhanna Gissova, as her sound technician, so their women's group was housed in the dormitory room. They lived and slept with the factory workers and filmed them every day. The material was terrific because they could show how well these girls lived, but every pixel of the screen showed the squalor of that life and told them otherwise.[43]

They filmed them with incredible sympathy. Goldowska had never seen such a flow of life on the screen before. After that the director was fired from his job, and Goldowska did not agree to re-mount the material and remained in her principled position. In the end the picture was burned, but she managed to make a copy of it and kept it at the Moscow State University. She remained faithful to her principles from her first films made as a director to her last: "Raisa Nemchinskaya - Circus Artist" (1970), "Deniska - Denis" (1976), "The Trial" (1978), "This Shaking World" (1994), "The Prince" (1999-2001). She has made all of her films using the "method of observation." She always tries to observe a person in life: first she gets to know him as intimately as possible, so that he can behave completely freely. Then she starts filming him; this often happens from the very first minutes. There is a set of techniques, and if you follow them, you can create a comfortable atmosphere for the person. If you establish a normal, friendly relationship with the person, then you can do whatever you want with him. This, above all, is the task of the relationship. By the way, Goldowska is also against the script. It's silly when they say you have to write a script. What is the script if we do not know how life will turn out.

"It means that you write one thing, but you do another, you're always deceiving someone. You're navigating between the possible and the impossible.[44]

It was not easy to uncover the living person in documentary filmmaking, but the directors made so many bright discoveries in the process. It was documentary filmmakers of this period that became more like what we have today. In most documentaries, the filmmakers strive to show a real person, to reveal the characteristics of their character and to make them close to the others. With the help of a hidden camera, filmmakers achieved a stunning effect. One of the sensational events was the film by V. Lisakovich's Katyusha (1964). The portrait of the film's heroine, a nurse scout Catherine Demina, was built around a single episode shot using the hidden camera method. Imagine what the heroine, sitting in the audience during the screening, felt when she suddenly saw herself and her front-line comrades on the screen.

---

[43] We need to look for an image, not information: Marina Goldovskaya on the search for a hero and the method of observation//T&R//15.10.2015//ЬЦp://1NeoguappbrgasCce.sh/ro818/7850-shagta-doYou8caua
[44] Ibid.

These feelings probably can't be shown by any shots. Such was also the film "Look at Your Face" (1966) by documentary filmmakers Pavel Kogan and Pyotr Mostovoy, based on a script by Sergei Solovyov. For many weeks, the camera filmed the faces of visitors to the Hermitage as they viewed Leonardo's Madonna Litta. Thus was born a story of man's encounter with the beautiful and the great power of art.

Another film that appeals to the people is "235,000,000" (1967). The wide-ranging film was made by Uldis Braun from a script by Hertz Frank and was dedicated to the 50th anniversary of Soviet power. The social order connected the living fates of 235 million people of different nationalities, social groups and professions. It was these people who gave real meaning to such concepts as homeland, nation and patriotism.

In the history of documentary filmmaking, filmmakers have faced ethical problems. The documentary filmmaker very often intrudes into people's lives. What are the limits of acceptability? One such controversial film was Gualtiero Iacopetti's A Dog's Life (1962). After this film was shown at the Cannes Film Festival, critics called it "a kaleidoscope of human abominations." The film showed pictures from different parts of the world: German alcoholics leaving night bars to sprawl home, in Southeast Asia, in restaurants, fresh street dogs to let them for stew, foodies eating live worms, a Buddhist monk burning himself in broad daylight in a crowded square. All of this was accompanied by a voice-over that only explained what the viewer saw on the screen. It is likely that the director did not want to scare the viewer with these shots, but simply wanted to show the other side of the world. He also wanted to show that people in the "atomic age" still have such wild instincts. Iacopetti has also been called by the press the pioneer of "documentary filmmaking. Iacopetti continued to make films in the same spirit after that. In his film Goodbye Africa (1965) he showed how, freed from colonial dependence, peoples pour out rivers of blood, beat each other, destroy nature, commit cult murders, etc. Critics particularly condemned him for his depiction of shootings. There were even rumors that Iacopetti himself paid executioners to get such footage.
Is there a justification for all this, or does it not matter what methods you use to get to the desired result?

Iacopetti had his own followers, but the attempts to create films in the same spirit were not so talented: "Faces of Death", which showed all kinds of death penalty, "Shocking Asia", which came out in 4 episodes. It also showed various religious rituals of South Asian peoples who live by the rules of primitive society, "love temples" for the realization of the most unrestrained sexual fantasies, sex-change operations, etc.

The intrusion into the lives of ordinary people requires documentary filmmakers to engage in constant ethical analysis. After all, if filmmakers finish their work and switch to another film, the people they filmed must still live with it in this life. The same can be said of journalists, who most often deal with human fates.

The very first such sensational experience of long-term observation was Craig Gilbert's. In the early 1970s he makes a 12-part film called American Family. The director was filming an ordinary Californian Laud family in the city of Santa Barbara. The film crew lived in a hotel that was next door to this family's home, who agreed to be filmed for free. For seven months, the director, along with the cameraman, would show up at their house every day at 6 a.m., where the camera was set up. During the long shoot a lot was going on in this family, such as almost starting a fire, or a lot was coming out: the hotel had a new mistress, the son went to New York and started living there with a homosexual, etc. The cameraman of course went after the son where he was going. The result was 300 hours of footage on film, from which the director edited 12 one-hour episodes. The episodes were shown weekly on television for three months. Audience reaction was violent and strongly negative. Many began to accuse the director of distorting and slandering an ordinary American family. The family, on the other hand, after watching the film initially admitted that everything in it was right, they are. But then, when the Lauds found out about the reaction of other people, they themselves began to accuse him too and even wanted to sue him for distorting the image of the family.

The same experience was done in England and they made a multi-part film called "Family. It was about the family of an ordinary bus driver who lived together with a lodger who rented a room from them. But this film differed from the other by the fact that the contractual series had to appear on the screen no later than three months after the start of filming. It turned out that the screening was already in parallel with the filming of new series. That is, it was a telling difference for television. After that, similar attempts were repeated several times. Hence began to appear series, which are now on television in huge numbers. But the essential difference in these soap operas is that they starred real people and families. All of this was more like reality TV, one of the most common and highest-rated genres on 21st-century television. To answer the question: why exactly such programs are unsurpassed success among viewers, we can answer simply that people like to watch real people in real life. It is this kind of non-staged and life-filled footage that makes movies and shows more entertaining and intriguing.

It should also be noted that after the release of the Gilbert film, the family broke up. It is hard to say whether or not it would have broken up without the film, but the fact remains that the filming contributed to the family's breakup more quickly. From this we must conclude that documentary filmmakers must bear at least some moral responsibility.

It all brought to mind a more recent film directed by Peter Weir, made in 1998. "The Truman Show" starring Jim Carrey, who won a Golden Globe for that role. The movie's tagline was "He's on live TV and doesn't even realize..." Truman suddenly realizes that everything around him is a set and people are actors who pretend to be what they just seem to be. His whole world turns out to be a big TV show, in which he plays the main role and does not even know it. His whole life, from the moment he was born, is the result of a TV show author watching the whole world.[45]

Among the significant Russian documentaries we should also mention "Anna: From Six to Eighteen," directed by Nikita Mikhalkov. In his film, he traces the history of Russia from 1980 to 1991, through the eyes of a child, asking his daughter such questions as what she loves most or what scares her.

Another such example is the film "Nika, which..." (1993) by Anatoly Borsyuk, a famous Kiev documentarian and TV presenter. He told about the poetess Nika Turbina, who became famous at the age of 8 for her poems. Then he made a movie about an adult Nika - the unlucky girl "Nika Turbina" (2000). Nika never became a famous poetess, fame as it came and went, and she threw herself out the window and hurt herself. When the second film premiered in 2001, during an interview, Anatoly Borsyuk said one phrase that may have been fateful for the girl: "She is 26 years old, her whole life is ahead of her, but it feels as if she has almost lived it to the end"[46] . In 2002, Nika did commit suicide. The director also made a third film, "Nika Turbina. The Last Flight." The film was shown at the Kiev house of cinema, but was not allowed on the screen anymore. The question arises whether her tragic fate was not the fault of the same poets and critics who patronized her, the documentary filmmakers

[45]   Kortunov P. Every time you watch TV, it looks at you// KinoCafe//
http://www.kinocafe.ru/reviews/?rid=61900
[46]   Glushenkov K. They didn't have to grow old///Nevskoe Vremya
//bcr://pu8rb.ru/81ope8/8O81agD8aua-1sh-pe-18Yo8-56024/?ueg8yun=rgt1

who addressed her fate?

Perhaps it is a matter of moral choice on the part of the documentary filmmaker. It's up to him to choose whether to film a fire, a fight, a drowning man, or to rush to help them.

CHAPTER 3. TELEVISION JOURNALISM

3.1 Formation and Development of the Genre Structure of Television Cinematography

Television is a set of devices that transmits moving images and sound over a distance. TV can also be described as an organization that produces and distributes television programs. It develops dynamically and never stands still. With its most powerful mechanisms for influencing public opinion, it is television that shapes the opinions and stereotypes of mass audiences and dictates their trends. It has had a great influence on the formation of the modern structure of mass communications and on its relationship with different social and cultural institutions. It has become an essential and indivisible part of everyday life, an element that fills leisure time. Television also gives people something that they need every day, namely information. It is a powerful source of everyday information.

With the advent and development of television, art, so to speak, came into our room. Its conflicting juxtaposition with everyday life has in no way diminished its emotional perception. Art had never before come so close to people in the immediate home environment. [47]

In addition to the rest of the older media, the emergence of television was also viewed ambiguously by documentary filmmakers. While at first many were jealous of television and thought it was a heavy blow to filmmaking, over time many gradually began to understand and see the future of documentary filmmaking in television. It has enormous possibilities for documenting reality. The boundaries of modern television production cannot be set at once, as it carries elements of various fields of art and performs numerous functions. In order to define its boundaries, it is necessary to understand which topics are of great interest to viewers. All over the world, viewers prefer to watch news, soap operas and comedy programs. In addition to those listed above, there is a great demand for documentaries and movies. Viewers always want to hear the news and see footage that portrays reality. Today, clear boundaries between different television genres are already being washed away. Many of them in their pure form are very rare. The form of existence of television is considered a program. In fact, television requires more simplified forms. Modern television production is designed for quick and easy perception by the audience. Everything here is very clear and

---

[47] Sappak V.Television and us. Conversation one M.: "Art",1988//NTsr:/^-#-#.euag118GpagotGyLeh112/85.N1sh

understandable.

Any television program realizes itself in the present, as it is always made with the expectation of a momentary perception, and sometimes even for a specific day and hour. This is compounded by the fact that video recording gives the impression of being, so to speak, broadcast. In order for television production to be effective and to have its own permanent defined audience, it is necessary to rethink already existing genre modifications, to fill them with additional content, and to apply them successfully in new modern conditions.[48]

Here we can talk about numerous video channels, which include television programs that extend over time, are linked together by unity of territorial and thematic nature, and have one or more well-known hosts. Such genres as music and entertainment shows, TV games ("What? Where? When?", "KVN"), talk shows, and a more complex form of television - TV film - are worth mentioning. The activity of the anchorman, who has a great responsibility to materialize the result of the joint work of all the creators of the program who remain behind the scenes, is of great importance.

Rapidly evolving television offers more and more new forms of realization of programs. For example, compared to traditional genres, talk shows are a newer genre, responding to great consumer demand. A relatively new genre in English means a talk show or conversational performance[49] . This genre earned widespread popularity with audiences in the 1960s, first in the United States and then in Western Europe and around the world. We spoke in more detail about this particular television genre because it contains the essential elements of both interview, discussion, and show. It is the talk show that more or less gives us a clear picture of modern television production. We see vivid examples of such programs today on both Russian and Armenian TV channels. Although talk shows on Armenian TV often do not address the urgent problems that the moderator, so to speak, must pose. This genre is also distinguished by the fact that, it often includes the possibility of connecting viewers to the conversation by telephone or speakerphone in the studio. Two-way dialogue between two different audiences is also possible, which is called "telebridge. Not only are journalists being formed as individuals, but there is also the possibility for the viewer, the ordinary people behind the screens, to be involved. Television is becoming more interactive.

Most recently, in the Armenian capital, Yerevan, there was a large-scale scientific and

---

[48]   Zubok A. S. Television business. School of Publishers and Media Without Borders. 2002., C. 228-229
[49]   Kuznetsov G. V., Tsvik V. L., Yurovsky A. Y. Television journalism. Chapter VIII. Genres of television journalism, 2002. //http://evartist.narod.ru/text6/32.htm

practical journalistic seminar called "Mediapoligon: Yerevan-24. I would like to mention this particular format of the modern journalistic project, because it involved the round-the-clock operational broadcasting of news from various points in the city. Thus, young students and journalists had a great opportunity to work in real time and gain great experience in prompt, accurate work. Especially lately, more and more new media are appearing on the Internet, and the format of presenting materials is changing. The role of text is gradually decreasing, and the emphasis is put more on photos, video and audio materials, statistics and other graphic means that do not take up much time from the consumer and provide the necessary concise and clear information. More and more multimedia options are emerging. Television has all the potential to provide information in a more vivid and interesting format.

With the transition of television (TV) broadcasting to digital standards, it soon became clear that the way for its further development is through the creation of high-speed, i.e. broadband networks. And then everyone started talking about the coming convergence of the Internet and TV, because the Internet is just such a broadband network. TV moguls were seized by the idea of offering interactive TV (ITV) in exchange for access to customers. TV companies rushed to create ITV projects from its simplest forms to the most complex. And it can be done exactly on the way of convergence with the Internet. Convergence here can be defined as a process that combines technologies and services into a flexible interactive service system, effectively serving the needs of consumers. [50]

And so, based on the above attributes, we can conclude that modern television production is characterized by the following characteristics:

- Speed
- Dynamism
- Fusion of genres
- Interactivity
- Immensity
- Documentary
- The ability to engage the viewer

It is worth noting that the television product is also documentary in nature. Even those reports that are made on television by journalists include documentary elements. They also

---

[50]   Zaitsev A. Convergence of the Internet and
TV//PCWEEK//08.1E2000//http://www.pcweek.ru/infrastructure/article/detail.php?ID=55951

reflect reality.

In analyzing the possibilities of television, we have come to the most expressive form of program presentation: the television film. A television film is a film that is made specifically for display on television. A television film is designed to be shown repeatedly along with other programs, but with the audience's interests and conditions of perception in mind. A key feature of television films is that they are most often multiple episodes. A TV documentary includes interviews, voice-over narration by the author, etc. In fact, a TV movie is very different from a classic documentary. There is a big risk here. Whereas the viewer watches a documentary selectively, the viewer of television looks at the screen arbitrarily. There is a risk that he may not even finish the film at all. That is why television must entice the viewer with its film any time he wants to look at the screen. It must keep the viewer engaged and intrigued throughout the film. The conclusion to be drawn from this is that you have to be constantly focused on the viewer: if the viewer is not interested, you don't need a television movie.

Nowadays, a genre that combines a purely documentary film with a reconstruction of various events has become very widespread in world TV.[51]

Although classic documentary filmmakers may resent it, this is the genre that has become prevalent in world television. The basis of the film is strictly documentary, but much is also acted out by actors. The first originators of reconstructed films were the BBC. They take diaries and real events, and on this basis, a film is made with the participation of actors, that is a complete reconstruction. The need for this appears when there is no documentary video footage of historical events. The rhythm of cinema is very different from that of television. In TV, everything develops in a dynamic way. Those who work in newsrooms feel this rhythm particularly well. You could say they have a constant counter in their heads. A film on television is made to the exact second.

Television film would not have happened without the work of directors M. Goldovskaya, I. Belyaev, I. Shadhan, V. Vinogradov, and others. In television documentaries, characters increasingly find themselves in conflict situations, forcing them to make difficult choices. This is especially evident in the late 1980s, beginning with M. Goldovskaya's Arkhangelskiy Muzhik.

---

[51] Chekmarev A. A. Teledocumentary as a format for society reflection // http://cyberleninka.rU/article/n/teledokumentalistika-kak-format-refleksii-obschestva

We would like to pay special attention to the TV channel "Culture", which is known for a large number of its documentary programs and films. One of the most striking and informative among them is the TV magazine "Absolute Hearing".[52]

The program is hosted by Gennady Yanin. It is designed for an audience that will be interested in a wide variety of musical genres and directions, from classical to pop music. In 2011, the program was awarded a diploma of participation in the finals of the TEFI 2011 National Television Competition. The program was also awarded a diploma of the All-Russian Festival of TV Programs and Films "TeleProfi" in the category "Educational Program". Kultura" TV channel also features special documentary series and programs: "Documentary Camera" - a series of programs about leading documentary filmmakers and documentary film by Andrei Shemyakin, "Seekers" - a documentary series of cognitive-adventure programs that tell stories about significant events in Russian history and not only, about private people who left behind many questions and mysteries, "Geniuses and Villains" - a series of portraits of prominent figures in world culture and science. Among the documentaries from the series "Islands" made in 2014 were also films about our great compatriots Sergei Paradjanov and Frunze Dovlatyan. The film about Paradzhanov begins with a shot of the studio and garden named after Alexander Dovzhenko, where there is a monument to the director Sergey Paradzhanov, whose three columns symbolize Armenia, Georgia, Ukraine and the Holy Trinity simultaneously, the center of the monument depicts the Virgin Mary, below the characters of his famous film "Shadows of Forgotten Ancestors" Ivan and Marichka, and crowns the composition with Paradzhanov's head. There are no voice-over narration in the film, but Roman Balayan, his friend and director, reminisces about Sergey Paradzhanov; the film also includes an interview with the hero himself. A film about Frunze Dovlatyan has the same relaxed narrative. Instead of a voice-over text about the heroes are told by contemporaries, shots from the archives are shown, where they themselves speak. Thus, the TV film has a freer and more natural character.

In Chapter 2 we discussed some cases in the history of filmmaking in which documentaries were turned into reality television shows. Thus, today one can see on television not only reality shows that are only entertaining and made for ratings, but also cognitive intellectual reality shows. Examples of such programs can be found again on the TV channel "Culture". The "Polyglot" program implies an intensive course of foreign language learning

---

[52]   Russia K. Absolute Hearing/LSHrU/TsKiiiga.gi/bgapy/zIohu/bgapy id/20892/

in 16 lessons. The teacher is a real polyglot Dmitry Petrov, who has more than 30 languages under his belt.

Television must also fulfill its functions: informational, educational, enlightening, and entertaining. It must take responsibility for what is shown. The great director of Spanish and Mexican origin, Luis Buñuel, believes that every art should have a mystery at its core, but the screen lacks it. Directors, screenwriters and producers try to shield people from anything that might upset them. They keep repeating the same drama to help people forget their everyday worries. And it's all repeated in terms of morality, religion, and censorship.

By saying all this, the director was referring to Hollywood entertainment films, which is not the case with documentary films, of course. After all, while other films, though by no means all of them, may be created just to entertain the viewer, documentaries are created precisely to show the truth, to go deeper into that truth, not to hide even the smallest details, sometimes even turning off all moral principles.

Technological advances can lead to changes in television documentary filmmaking for the better. The film production process is becoming cheaper, and different TV channels are beginning to produce documentaries in large numbers. As a result, a competitive environment is developing between the various TV channels. It is hoped that from this huge number a better product will be selected by people who are interested. Documentary films on television have already received a permanent residence permit, even in a simplified version. Both television and documentary filmmakers benefit, gaining a certain target audience.

We have talked about the features of the television film, because the journalistic genres are also related to it. In informational, analytical, and artistic genres the elements of documentary, non-fiction, and factual material are considered.For example, fiction journalism uses an imaginative reflection of reality, but this image is taken from non-fiction, factual material.

Today it is very common for a television screen to be swapped for a monitor screen. Because it is convergence, and the creation of many Internet television stations, that is changing the format of modern television production. The documentary has gone beyond the television screen. Web documentaries (webdocs) or simply interactive films are now becoming popular[53] . This genre involves the multimedia narration of history on the Internet.

---

[53] Web documentary: interactive movies on the Internet//onMedia//http://onmedia.dw-akademie.com/russian/?p=399 3

But the main distinguishing feature of such films is the great involvement of the audience. The latter can choose the fragments they are interested in and change the drama of the story. They become a co-author of the film. The viewer, for example, chooses in what form to watch the interview with the main character - video or audio, accompanied with various illustrations. He has the opportunity to add his comments, to participate in an interactive voting. The work of creating a web documentary involves not only the author, but also the designer, photographer, programmer and web developer. If, for example, it takes 10 days to shoot a film, the programming takes twice as long. Interactive films are most engaged in such famous Internet publications as The New York Times, for example. In Armenia, it is still too early to talk about the web documentary phenomenon. But in Russia, it is already
there are several online publications dealing with interactive projects.
For example, one such project was done on the Lenta.ru website.

3.2. Cinematic language in TV journalism: reportage, interview, essay

An integral part of modern television production is good old-fashioned reporting, which does not lose its relevance and always keeps up with the latest television trends. The reportage genre is the most widespread, effective and leading in television journalism, as well as in documentary filmmaking. The term reportage means to report. This genre is used on television by journalists to promptly report on an event or incident, of which the correspondent himself is a participant. The functions of reporting are now known to any consumer of information, but reporting, as an important part of modern television production, realizes its functions and possibilities in a completely different direction. Today reportage is the embodiment of mobility, speed and relevance, which perfectly characterizes modern television production. In addition to fixed reports, live on-the-spot reporting is also common. It is necessary to take into account the interests of the audience, which are satisfied with reliable, live, up-to-date news. We see how the rhythm of life is changing. Today, it is not enough just to sit in the newsroom or the newsroom and wait for the news to come out. You have to be mobile. The recent reports from our compatriots on the hot spots during the tragic and bitter clashes between Nagorno-Karabakh and Azerbaijan are a vivid example of this. During the 4-day war the journalists tried to cover the news as swiftly and authentically as possible. It is scary for the average citizen to sit at home and watch the reports, where the shots from the enemy's side are heard in the frame, and the journalist is literally just a few steps away from the hot spots. All of this characterizes modern television production, which must arouse the audience's interest and be exciting. Here it is also appropriate to recall the front-line cameramen and directors who dedicated their lives to filming on the front lines, being with the brave heroes of war, the defenders of the fatherland. As mentioned already in the part of the work that told about the Armenian cinematography, one of those directors is our contemporary Vardan Hovhannisyan. The director became famous for his film "Stories of People at War and in Peace", telling about the Karabakh war.

And so, it is in television journalism reports that the elements of documentary are most considered. Simple reports can sometimes even turn into TV films. This depends on the journalistic work and on the editing, of course, if we are talking about a staged report. Live footage shot on the spot of an incident can serve as newsreel for a more serious documentary. Both reportage and documentary film have the same goal: to show the viewer the real facts, not to make up anything, not to exaggerate, to fix reality.

Alexander Kolesnichenko writes in his book "Practical Journalism" that if reporting is a purely informational genre, it does not mean that the reporter at the scene should be emotionless. On the contrary, the journalist must experience them and show them in the reportage. In order for the report to interest the viewer, the journalist must show in it a new aspect of the event - a side of the subject unknown to the viewer. And we must also remember that people are always at the center of the reportage, and a special place in the preparation of the reportage is given to communication with people. [54]

Interviews are considered an integral part not only of television journalism, but also of television film. A journalist gets the information he or she needs first and foremost by talking to different people. The word interview in English means a meeting, a conversation. The television interview is characterized by its spectacularity, which explains the particular credibility and widespread use of the genre in various television programs. It can be stated out loud that 90% of TV movies are interviews. As already experienced interviewers note, in order to get to the underlying characteristics of the interlocutor, it is necessary to show great interest and to be mentally attuned. To recall Marina Goldovskaya's words, she is a proponent of a long observation of a person in life. An experienced documentary filmmaker first gets to know the person, establishes a friendly relationship with him and creates a comfortable

---

[54] Kolesnichenko A. V. Practical journalism. Moscow: Moscow University, 2013. C. 51-52

environment for him, after which he already begins to film him and ask his questions. The interviewee begins to behave more naturally and casually in front of the camera. Accordingly, the answers are also sincere and evoke reciprocal feelings in the viewer.

If we contradict the long-standing system of television journalism, we can cite the American Flaherty cameraman Richard Leacock, of whom we spoke above, as an example. In the 1950s and 1960s, he himself improved the quality of the camera so that reporters could get interviews under any circumstances.However, when he saw that journalists were almost forcing unfortunate interviewees to swallow the microphone while shooting, he realized that he had created a real monster. In his opinion, not one word of the person in front of the camera should be believed. The best way is to observe him at work. But today's rhythm of television does not allow for slow work. There is hardly a single newscast on TV today that does not include short synchronicities of some competent person involved in some event or other. Most often, interviews are used when the interviewee's words sound more expressive and significant than the journalist's voice-over narration. Most often portrait interviews are used in feature films and documentaries. It is the portrait interview that can become a document of time, corresponding to the image of an entire generation. A person may not even talk about himself, but his personality is still revealed in a set of moral principles.

Maria Lukina explains the mechanism of the journalistic interview in her book "Interview Technology". First of all, you need to divide the interview work into three stages: preparation, conducting and completion. You need to clearly define goals and objectives, research information about your character, think through basic questions, interview strategy and of course make first contact with your interlocutor. You should also leave extra time for unplanned questions and answers and prepare for the most unexpected situations. [55]

The formula for a successful interview lies in the journalist's ability to ask questions professionally. However, the interview also includes equally important verbal components. After all, how does an interview begin? By saying a few etiquette phrases and establishing rapport. It is also important to find the right way to develop the conversation. The journalist must "find the key" to his interlocutor, that is, find the right approach to him or be able to "feel" his interlocutor.

One of the genres of fiction journalism, the essay, is also closer to documentary

---

[55]   Lukina M. M. Interview technology. M.: Aspect Press. 2005. C. 30-37, 49

filmmaking. Due to the fact that this genre is the richest in its pictorial means, it is closely associated with cinema art. This genre is often referred to as a frontier genre.[56]

On the one hand the essay reflects real facts and events, on the other hand it requires talent, creativity and professionalism from the author. The essay combines the study of documentary material with a story. It has a strictly documentary basis (real characters and circumstances, non-fictional facts, etc.), but at the same time is characterized by figurative characteristics and a special compositional structure. It is particularly close to dramatic works. The main difference between the essay and the reportage is that the focus here is already on the person as the subject of the action. The essay, as well as the documentary, may use not only portrait interviews, but also archival footage, long observations, hidden camera, etc.

Consequently, the essay does not simply talk about a subject, but gives a clear analysis of the author. The author, like the film director, uses his imagination and cameraman's ingenuity. Often the method of prolonged observation is also used, which is a characteristic feature of documentary film.

---

[56] Kuznetsov G. V., Tsvik V. L., Yurovsky A. Y. Television journalism. Chapter VIII. Genres of TV journalism, 2002. //http://evartist.narod.ru/text6/32.htm

The final result of our study is the report film. But before we present it, we would like to address the perennial problem of the script, which has been a controversial subject of heated discussion among various directors and screenwriters over the years. Some have been in favor of a script being necessary to make a film, while others have found it completely pointless to write a script before starting the filmmaking process. In this regard, we were reminded of a wager by the famous screenwriter Tonino Guerra, who bet with the iconic director Federico Fellini that he could come up with a complete movie 10 seconds long. The next day, he brought a finished film plot, where a woman looks at the TV screen, and there is a broadcast of a rocket launch. There is a countdown: 10...,9...,8... Her face is shown, showing a storm of worry. And in the final seconds she picks up the phone, dials a number, and as the rocket launches, she says into the receiver: "Prezzay, he's gone." Thus, the screenwriter composed the script for the shortest movie in the history of cinema. Another case is Federico Fellini's famous film "8 and a Half", where the main character Guido, who is the director himself, does not enlighten anyone with his idea for a new film: the actors and sets are ready, but no one clearly knows even his role. The director wants in this way to show his way from a dead end to a story with a groundbreaking view of cinema.

Other filmmakers have also addressed the question of the script. In most cases, documentary filmmakers oppose the script, believing that documentary filmmaking is the most unforeseeable kind of filmmaking. The crew never knows how drastically reality can change. Directors John Grierson and Robert Flaherty also argued about the script. The first insisted that the film needed an "ironclad script," while the second, on the contrary, said that life itself would write the script. Filmmakers become powerless in the face of reality. A confirmation of the above, as we mentioned in the second chapter of our study, was the screenplay for Industrial Britain by Robert Flaherty. Incidentally, he co-directed the film with Grierson. There was only one phrase in the script: "The film will consist of pictures of industrial Britain.

Dziga Vertov also radically denied the need for a screenplay. He went even further in the argument about the script by declaring in the credits of his famous film "The Man with the Camera" that the film had no script.

If we continue the list of those who were against the script, we can also remember

Marina Goldovskaya. The director talked about how writing a script is stupid. "It means that you write one thing, but do another, all the time deceiving someone. Navigating between the possible and the impossible."

If we consider this problem from a different angle, we can say that in the history of cinema there have often appeared adaptations of literary works. It turns out that these same works served as a script for directors. Almost all the works of the great Fyodor Mikhailovich Dostoyevsky were adapted: "The Idiot," "The Double," "Crime and Punishment," "The Funny Man's Dream," "The Brothers Karamazovs," "The Possessed," etc. The easy film adaptation of all these works is related to the clear form in which the writer builds the plot of his works. He seems to have already had the finished plot of the work in his head before he wrote it. As René Clair used to say, "The movie is ready - all that's left is to shoot it. In the works of Dostoevsky all the details are thought out to the smallest detail, there is nothing superfluous in the plot. Here it is appropriate to recall the words of Anton Chekhov, that if in the first act of a play there is a gun hanging on the wall, then in the last act it should definitely go off.

Based on the above professional opinions, we came to the conclusion that life itself writes the script of the documentary. In any case, something may change on the set, and a written text will not save it. So the script of our film is a kind of opposition to all the ideas and concepts of the great screenwriters and directors, who considered the existence of a script as necessary.

Our report film is based on the work done by a journalism student over a period of three years. We show footage of the journey, without exaggerating or minimizing even the smallest details. In the reportage of our research we show everything as it is: the made reports of different kinds of events, whether they are exhibitions of modern artists or meetings with ambassadors of different countries, scientific conferences, conclusion of important contracts, synchronisms, which also include a wide range of people, from students to professors, artists such as Bruno Bruni, etc. There's a lot to be accomplished in 3 years of intensive hands-on work. The film demonstrates the journalist's work on and off camera. Different stand-ups are shown, a lot of questions are asked which need answers: where and how the off-screen text can be used, how to combine the journalist's words with the footage, how to find the right background, to use elements of a documentary or a TV film, where it is better not to fill the entire space with words and where it is better to remain silent. But the main goal of our reporting film is to show how a future journalist can reach his or her author's program, and by learning from his or her own mistakes, starting with simple reports, gradually complicate them and improve. The name of the author's program is "Profession - Man". At the center of the program are various famous and little-known figures of art and science. But the aim of the journalist is not to reveal the peculiarities of their work, but to reveal the personality of the person through various questions and to show that human qualities are in the first place, no matter how much the person sitting opposite you is a recognized professional.

CONCLUSION

Based on the theoretical part of our study, we were convinced that documentary filmmaking has more to do with television and journalism than we thought. In order to identify the characteristic features of modern television film, it took us a long study of cinematography since its birth, as well as a study of the specifics of television and journalistic work.

During our research we have studied the stages of the formation of documentary cinema on the example of films by foreign, Soviet, Russian and Armenian directors. It turned out that, due to technological advances, documentary filmmaking developed in a completely different direction and began to meet the needs of different target audiences. As a result, television film gradually began to take shape. In the course of our work, we made some interesting observations: a significant fact is the fact that in modern television movies, not only frames from old newsreels, but also frames from famous feature films are very often used. If, for example, the picture is about an actor, then the frames of those feature films where he played are used. Hence, it follows that the TV movie also uses elements of feature films. Further we came to the conclusion that in order to reveal to the viewer the personality of the hero of the TV film, the emphasis is more on interviews with his loved ones, or colleagues and various professionals. The peculiarity of the majority of modern TV films is that the offscreen text of the journalist gives way to a live interview, or the hero himself tells his story in front of the camera. We would also like to mention the TV channel "Kultura", which is distinguished by its widest range of documentary programs and cycles, and specializes in programs about Russian and world history, science, literature, art, etc. The production of its own documentaries is known for the BBC, which, as it turns out, is the pioneer of television reconstructions of films.

Our research has shown that documentary film not only has a close relationship with journalism, but is also a mass medium.

Based on the results of our research work, we argue that the role of the journalist in the creation of a documentary film is very important and great. During the filming process, the journalist must pay attention to the following:

- Always keep in mind that circumstances on the set can change dramatically, therefore, you should always remember that the documentary film is the most unpredictable type of cinematography, because it is based on real life.

- Teamwork is very important. First of all, the journalist must coordinate his actions with the cameraman, quickly concentrate, not to miss the moment and capture the shot.
- The journalist must know his hero very well. Be able to communicate with him and establish a friendly relationship, create a comfortable environment for him and only then begin to ask his questions and expect sincere answers.
- You need to have a ready-made scenario in your head and think montage-wise.
- If you make a documentary, it does not mean that the author should not include his imagination and use artistic expressive means in it as well.

In our research paper, we took a closer look at several journalistic genres (reportage, interview, essay) and found that they include important documentary elements.

We have also studied Armenian documentary filmmaking and came to the conclusion that we have many talented directors who have made their own special contribution to the development of not only Armenian, but also world cinematography. A striking example of this is our contemporary Vardan Hovhannisyan's much acclaimed film, "Stories of People in War and Peace. Today, we also have the Golden Apricot International Film Festival, whose founder is the famous documentary filmmaker Harutyun Khachatryan.

Thus, we have seen that documentary film plays an essential role in capturing reality. On modern television it can be a powerful means for a journalist to reveal important phenomena of reality, can bring to the viewer deep truth and most often show what people are unable to see for themselves. However, the author of a documentary must never forget the moral principles: the documentary he or she creates can have irreversible consequences and become fateful for the hero of the film.

LIST OF REFERENCES

Scientific and educational literature

1. Bakhtin. M. Problems of Dostoevsky's Poetics. Moscow: Art Literature, 1963.

2. Dziga V. Articles, diaries, plans. Moscow: Art, 1966 - 320 p.

3. Goldovskaya M. E. Man close-up, Moscow: Art, 1981.

4. Zubok A. S. Television business. School of publishing and media beznesa. 2002 - 560 c.

5. Kalantar K. L. Amo Bek-nazarov. E.: "Ayastan", 1973 - 167 p.

6. Kolesnichenko A. V. Practical journalism. Moscow: Moscow University, 2013 - 191 p.

7. Kuleshov L. The ABC of Film Direction, Moscow: "Art", 1969 - 132 p.

8. Kukarkin A. V. Charlie Chaplin. Moscow: "Art", 1960 - 321 p.

9. Lukina M. M. Technology of interview. M.: Aspect Press, 2005 - 192 p.

10. Muratov S. Moral principles of TV journalism. Moscow, 1995 - 55 p.

11. Peleshyan A. My Cinema. E.: "Sovetskan Groh", 1988 - 256 p.

12. Sadoul J. General History of Cinema. Volume 1. Moscow: "Art", 1958.

13. Freilich S. I. Film Theory: from Eisenstein to Tarkovsky. Moscow: Academic Project: Alma Mater, 2005 - 512 p.

14. Eisenstein in Memoirs of Contemporaries. Moscow: "Art", 1974 - 414 p.

Electronic sources

1. Georgie Gerzina Powells: Street photography is made fascinating by life itself// Ko8Ryo1o.com,08.12.2015//http://www.rosphoto.com/interview/dzhordzhi

   dzherzina pauels-4221

2. Kuznetsov G. V., Tsvik V. L., Yurovsky A. Y. Television journalism. Chapter VIII. Genres of TV journalism, 2002.

//http://evartist.narod.ru/text6/32.htm

3. Hollywood pioneer Ruben Mamulyan from Tbilisi//Yo7oz1|YK//19.03.2016// http://novostink.ru/diaspora/148830-gollivudskiy-pioner-ruben-mamulyan-iz-tbilisi.html//11:40

4. Belinsky V.G. Vzglyad na russkoy literatury. On the Russian Novel and the Novels of Gogol, Sovremennik, 1988.

//http://az.lib.ru/b/belinskij w g/text 0320.shtml

5. Encyclopedia Krugosvet. Documentary Film. Founders// http://www.krugosvet.ru/enc/kultura i obrazovanie/theatr i kino/DOKUMENTA LNOE KINO.html?page=0,1

6. Vertov D. We//Theatre//#8, 2012//http://oteatre.info/my-variant-manifesta/

7. Laifurov. A. Words are nothing more 3Ha4ar//Interview//01.07.2014,15:34// http://www.interviewrussia.ru/movie/godfri-redzhio-slova-bolshe-nichego-ne-znachat?page=7

8. Hakobyan G. Harutyun Khachatryan: No one is not interested in why people run away and come back/Aravot//05.04.2013, 11:43 //http://ru.aravot.am/2013/04/05/154609/

9. The film "People's Stories of War and Peace" will be released in Armenia on 12 May//Armenia News//11.05.2011,14:32//http://newsarmenia.am/news/culture /culture-20110511-42451347/

10. Pozner V. V. Farewell to Illusions, 2015//http://www.litres.ru/vladimir-pozner/proschanie-s-illuziyami/chitat-onlayn/

11. Posner about Armenians: They are already older at birth than I will be at the hour of my death//Aysor//15.17.03,15:24//http://www.Y.aysor.am/ru/news/2013/07/15/vladimi r-pozner-about-armenians/641638

12. We need to look for an image, not information: Marina Goldovskaya on the search

for a hero and the method of observation/T&P//15.10.2015//http://theoryandpractice.ru/posts/7850- <u>marina-goldovskaya</u>

13. Sappak V. Television and Us. Conversation One. Moscow: "Art",1988// http://www.evartist.narod.ru/text12/85.htm

14. Zaitsev A. Convergence of Internet and TV//PCWEEK//08.11.2000//http://www.pcweek.ru/infrastructure/article /detail.php?ID=55951

15. Russia K. Absolute cayx//http://tvkultura.ru/brand/show/brand id/20892/

16. Siegfried K. The Nature of Film. Rehabilitation of Physical Reality. C. 6061// http://7lafa.com/book.php?id=78182&page=61

17. Glushenkov K. They did not have to grow old///Nevskoe Vremya//http://nvspb.ru/stories/sostaritsya-im-ne-prishlos-56024/?version=print

18. Web documentary: interactive films on the Internet//onMedia//http://onmedia.dw-akademie.com/russian/?p=399 3

19. Chekmarev A. A. Teledocumentary as a format for society reflection // http://cyberleninka.ru/article/n/teledokumentalistika-kak-format-refleksii- obschestva

Movies

1. "Amarcord. 1973. Italy. Directed by Federico Fellini
2. "8 and a Half." 1963. Great Britain. Directed by. Federico Fellini
3. "Battleship Potemkin. 1925. USSR. Directed by Sergey Eisenstein
4. "The Man with the Camera." 1929. Kiev. Directed by. Dziga Vertov.
5. "We." 1969. USSR. Director. Artavazd Peleshyan
6. "Inception. 1967. USSR. Director. Artavazd Peleshyan
7. "Stories of Men in War and Peace. 2007. Armenia. Director. Vardan Hovhannisyan
8. "The Truman Show. 1998. USA. Directed by. Peter Weir
9. "Russia K". Cycle of documentaries "Islands". "Frunze Dovlatyan", "Sergey Paradzhanov".
10. "Armenians, Forgive Us." 2009. Armenia. Director. Artem Yerkanyan

Printed by Books on Demand GmbH, Norderstedt / Germany